MW00386915

BEYOND
BROKEBACK

BEYOND
BROKEBACK
The Impact of a Film

Members of
The Ultimate Brokeback Forum

WingSpan Press
Livermore, California

Copyright © 2007 by Dave Cullen Forums
davecullen.com/forum/
All rights reserved.

No part of this book may be used or reproduced in any manner without written
permission of the copyright owner, except for brief quotations used in reviews
and critiques.

Printed in the United States of America

Published by WingSpan Press, Livermore, CA
www.wingspanpress.com

The WingSpan name, logo and colophon are the trademarks of
WingSpan Publishing.

ISBN 1-978-59594-122-0

First edition 2007

Library of Congress Control Number 2007924402

For Jack and Ennis

CONTENTS

ILLUSTRATIONS

Captions selected by Lucas Ginn from Annie Proulx, Larry McMurtry, and Diana Ossana. *Brokeback Mountain: Story to Screenplay*. New York: Scribner, 2005.

Acknowledgements

WITH SPECIAL THANKS TO

Leadership Team

Managing Editor - Lydia Wells Sledge, *KittyHawk*, Frankfort, Kentucky
Senior Editor - Jonathan Mortimer, *jlm1*, Sacramento, California
Editorial Advisor - Kathy Nolan, *kmich*, Detroit, Michigan
Research Team Leader - Ed Moore, *BigEd*, Vancouver, British Columbia, Canada
Art Director: Cover, Illustrations - K. M. Hill, *Brokebackbeauty*, Halifax, Nova Scotia, Canada

Editorial Team

Tina Adler, *DeTina*, Cabin John, Maryland
Kim E., *Elvan*, Sweden
Michael Elia, *Namdak*, Las Vegas, Nevada
Joseph L. Ellington, *goaboydc*, Alexandria, Virginia
Charlotte S. Graham-Clark, *royandronnie*, Virginia Beach, Virginia
Vicky Hartell, *VickyOuk*, London, United Kingdom
Jackie, *paintedshoes*, USA
Wayne D. Johnson, *wdj*, Atlanta, Georgia
Betty Greene Salwak, *neatfreak*, Indianapolis, Indiana
Archbishop Bruce J. Simpson, OSJB, *archbishop*, Wilkes Barre, Pennsylvania
Marcia Elvidge Smith, *Marge_Innavera*, Holden, Missouri
Trish Sisson Soulen, *Jaysmommy*, Minneapolis, Minnesota
John, *Desperadum*, New York, New York
Marleen Whiteley, *Tammy*, Västerås, Sweden

Design Team

Graphics - Chris Lattanzio, *ChrisTeva*, Staten Island, New York
Graphics Consultation - Sheera Duerigen, *trascedenza*, Novato, California
Graphics Captioning - H. Lucas Ginn, *DCLuke*, Washington, DC
Layout Design - Carol Viescas
Layout Design - Martina Glanzl, *desertrat*, Vienna, Austria

Research Team

Jeanine Byers, *lowcountrygirl*, Savannah, Georgia
Dan Campbell, *dcampbell01*, Somers Point, New Jersey
Kim E., *Elvan*, Sweden
Debra Garceau-McGarry, *Poohbunn*, Providence, Rhode Island
How Xian Neng, *Zuraffo*, Kuala Lumpur, Malaysia
Charlotte S. Graham-Clark, *royandronnie*, Virginia Beach, Virginia
Steve Hansen, *NWWaguy*, Ferndale, Washington
Bob Harris, *maturben*, Rochester, New York
Vicky Hartell, *VickyOuk*, London, United Kingdom
Garry L. Hunsaker, *Garry_LH*, Mexico, Missouri
Jackie, *paintedshoes*, USA

Jari Koskisuu, *Boris*, Helsinki, Finland
John La Fleur, *prjohn*, Phoenix, Arizona
Lisa Maguire, *LisaM*, Berlin, New Jersey
Mindy Moore, *MindyM*, Los Angeles, California
A. J. Morgan, *Jakelikethat*, Toronto, Ontario, Canada
Robert Parker, *Bobby19in1963*, Phoenix, Arizona
Pierre, New York, New York
Jack Schilling, *brokeback_1*, Denver, Colorado
secretme, France
Archbishop Bruce J. Simpson, OSJB, *archbishop*, Wilkes Barre, Pennsylvania
Tony, *Bbm-mmm*, Europe
Trish Sisson Soulen, *Jaysmommy*, Minneapolis, Minnesota
Conny Voesenek, *conny*, IJmuiden, Netherlands
Paulette Young, *berdache1*, Baltimore, Maryland

Permissions

Alice Akunyili, *Brokaholic*, Ontario, California
Kim E., *Elran*, Sweden

Biographies Team

Coordinator: Elle, *elle_ann*, Cape Town, South Africa
Bobby, *Bobby19in1963*, Phoenix, Arizona
Monica, *LoveEmBoys*, Berthoud, Colorado
Phil Day, *Pwday*, Kirkland, Washington
Gonzalo Gonzalez, *twistedboy*, Galveston, Texas
Jack Schilling, *brokeback_1*, Denver, Colorado
Dan Stafford, *trubrokeback*, Middletown, Ohio

Photography Contributions

Rob Freeman, *rob1318*, Bragg Creek, Alberta, Canada
Jim Bond, *In Tears*, Las Vegas, Nevada
Barry Gilligan, *csean97*, Uniontown, Ohio
Steve Gin, *Calgary Actor*, Calgary, Alberta, Canada
Dave Koerner, *Cowboy Dave*, Flagstaff, Arizona
Chris Lattanzio, *CrisFewa*, Staten Island, New York
Bob Sohomuch, *nora20194*, Reston, Virginia

The Daily Sheet Editors

Jan Geyer, *CactusGal*, Las Cruces, New Mexico
Ellen Raff, *tellyouwhat*, Dallas, Texas
Kathy Nolan, *kmich*, Detroit, Michigan
Elle, *elle_anne*, Cape Town, South Africa
Marcia, *Marge_Innavera*, Holden, Missouri

Book Marketing Team

Pat, *Pat Sinnot*, Dallas, Texas
Martina Glanzl, *desertrat*, Vienna, Austria
Monica, *LoveEmBoys*, Berthoud, Colorado

THE ULTIMATE BROKEBACK WEBSITES

Senior Managers and Advisory Board

Forum Founder/Owner - Dave Cullen, Denver, Colorado
Chief Moderator - *Melisande*, San Francisco, California
Technical Director - Greg Smith, *Parenthetical Greg*, San Francisco, California
Deputy Chief Moderator - Linda Andrews, *Killersmom*, San Antonio, Texas

Moderators

Adrian, North Vancouver, British Columbia, Canada
Bobbie, Virginia
K. M. Hill, *Brokebackbeauty*, Halifax, Nova Scotia, Canada
Brokeback1-J, New York, New York
Glenn, *BrokenOkie*, Oklahoma
Carissa, Long Island, New York
Caroline, Toronto, Ontario, Canada
Chuck DiGuilio, *CellarDweller115*, New Jersey
John, *Desperadum*, New York, New York
Esteban, *Estefue*, Central Coast of California
Fritz, *Fritzkep*, Arlingotn, Virginia
Heidi Skjordahl, *ImJackshesEnnis*, Indianapolis, Indiana
jim ... , upstate New York
Lance, Florida
Laurentia, Sweden
Lynn, Philadelphia, Pennsylvania
Mary, San Diego, California
Michael Flanagan, *michaelflanagansf*, San Francisco, California
Nick Fuller, *Nick_F*, Colchester, United Kingdom
Sandy Steever, *Sandy*, New Canaan, Connecticut
Sid Melucci, *Sid401K*, Oakland, California

Technical Team

John Trudell, *BayCityJohn*, Bay City, Michigan
Martina Glanzl, *desertrat*, Vienna, Austria
Monica, *LoveEmBoys*, Berthoud, Colorado
Gonzalo Gonzales, *twistedboy*, Galveston, Texas

VISIT OUR ONLINE COMMUNITIES

DaveCullen.com/Brokeback/book
DaveCullen.com/Brokeback/guide
DaveCullen.com/Forum/
FindingBrokeback.com
TheBrokebackTruck.ca

Editor's Note:

Some authors prefer to retain their anonymity and are identified in this book only by their screen names. Additional biographical information on many authors and book volunteers can be found at http://www.DaveCullen.com/brokeback/book/bios.

Beyond B R O K E B A C K

PREFACE

The short story hurt, and I read it completely alone. I saw the film two months later, in a huge theater, in the dark. I was surrounded. Hundreds of people gasped at the same moments with me. I heard them sobbing all around me; some were still tearing up in the lobby when it was all over. What happened to all those people? What did they do when they got home? Cry for another hour, go to sleep and forget it? Or wake the next morning, pick up the phone and make a change? Or did it gnaw away inside them for weeks until they figured out what they had to do?

We never get to see what happens. We know books and films can change lives; we've all seen it happen. We've seen it in our own lives, and occasionally we witness it with a friend. But what about all those other people who watched the remarkable film with us in the dark?

More than ten million people went to see *Brokeback Mountain* in the winter of 2005. For some of them it was just a movie. But others walked out of the theater feeling something ripped open inside them. They talked to friends, to family, to roommates, to therapists—some found what they needed there, others kept on looking. Thousands found each other on a website called The Ultimate Brokeback Forum. Some came to the site to discuss the film, others needed to talk about themselves. Some of us had seen a little more of ourselves on the screen than we were comfortable with. Even before the film's release, it started. The trailer called us on some of our bullshit. "There are lies we have to tell," one of the captions read. "There are truths we can't deny."

Lies we have to tell. Do we? When did we accept that, and what price did we pay? Jack and Ennis paid pretty dearly, and watching them swallow their lies was what it finally took for some people. Many of us left the theater fired up - something had to change, and this time it would. Many of us—we'll never know how many—slept on it and thought better of it. Maybe they could live with those lies. But we couldn't shake this film. It ate at us for days or weeks, it demanded change and it wasn't going away.

One of my biggest surprises was seeing how many Forum members lost weight. Or quit smoking. The changes weren't all earth-shattering, but twenty pounds or a clean set of lungs can make the day look a whole lot brighter. And these changes were often confidence boosters for an over-due plunge back into the dating pool. Quite a few members had something more drastic in mind. Several reconnected with lovers from their youth. Others faced the reality of divorce.

And a whole lot realized how lucky they were in their loving relationships and vowed to quit taking them for granted.

People made their way to the Forum for wildly divergent reasons. Some just needed to express their joy or catharsis or the stabbing pain in their gut. Openly, candidly, publicly, on a website. And some of them needed a little help. You don't end a marriage on a whim. And you can't talk your problem through with the people closest to you when you've been hiding it from them for twenty years. We had people hash their situation out for weeks with other members before they found the courage or the clarity to make a move.

The forum drew more than half a million posts in its first year, but the more startling figure concerns all the people who didn't post. Fifty to a hundred thousand came by each month just to silently witness. They had a unique position to watch from. Thousands of lives changed before our eyes on this Forum. First we shared the fictional lives—Jack and Ennis getting ripped apart on the screen in the dark. Then we saw what those guys did to us. Not just the immediate reaction in the lobby or over drinks an hour later, the lasting effect, months down the road—who changed, who didn't, with all the unexpected turns in our own stories.

So many changes—I never foresaw that. I wish I could say I created The Ultimate Brokeback Forum to help all those people. It never crossed my mind. Never occurred to me that they would need it. The intensity of the fallout from this film took me by surprise.

I started the website just to help the film. I had the feeling *Brokeback* was going to be groundbreaking, but I was convinced it would be stuck breaking that ground in the arthouse ghetto. Playing mostly to the converted. Assuming it stayed true to the short story, the film wasn't going to preach to anyone, but it was going to confront audiences with a situation that had escaped their attention for too long. Viewers could decide what they wanted about the predicament, but it was time they stopped ignoring it. Yet it seemed a safe bet that the mainstream would ignore the film. I knew the web had a lot of power to spread the word. So . . .

It started as a blog post. September 10, 2005. "*Brokeback* won Venice!" Wow. Venice is the most prestigious film festival in Europe. Winning that meant the film was no stinker. Maybe the big one we had been waiting for. Finally a film about gay guys that would speak to straight people. Speak to them in a voice they could handle. A great director, real Hollywood stars. "Could be a major pop culture moment," I wrote. "Gay cowboys in love. Hard to beat that. And two rising stars in Hollywood kissing. Can't wait."

I posted a dozen times over the several weeks, and comments started trickling in. Word was starting to spread. A little. On September 25, I created a separate web page dedicated to the film: release dates, links to early news stories and reviews, web sites featuring pictures of the actors, a plot summary, selected passages from the book . . . everything I could think of. And I made a central comments thread for readers to discuss the film. Most of my blog entries on *Brokeback* had drawn a handful of comments, but they were stranded in separate threads—one thread for each post. I figured if I linked back to one central thread every time I blogged about *Brokeback*, people might find each other more easily and get a discussion going. It was totally an afterthought. It would prove to be the most valuable thing I would ever post on my blog.

The comments thread on my blog holds roughly 120-150 posts. It took nearly two months to fill the first thread. The second took just four days: November 18-22. On December 9, *Brokeback Mountain* opened in five theaters in New York, Los Angeles and San Francisco. Our ninth comment thread filled up in a day and a half. Two weeks later, on Christmas Eve, we closed our fifty-sixth, and last thread, and directed the burgeoning community to our discussion-board website which eventually became known as The Ultimate Brokeback Forum.

The audience at the site was growing exponentially and I knew something had to give, but I didn't see a way out. In my daydreams I imagined a real discussion-board site, but laughed the idea off. That would require a team of programmers - way more than I could handle. I had a book contract of my own to fulfill. But on December 16, a poster from San Francisco named Melisande emailed with a suggestion. "I've been reading the message board at your blog for, jeez, has it been only a week?" she wrote. "And I'm thinking, it could be a real message board. Organized, in categories, with posters able to edit their posts and find the subjects that interest them. Right now it's a free-for-all, and it's great, but it could be better. I'm thinking topics could be The Movie with subthreads of Actors, Script, Awards, etc., then another topic on The Original Story, and - oh, hell, I'm just typing off the top of my head. A Personal Experience thread, with, e.g., My Ennis." It wouldn't be hard at all, she assured me—software packages were available for a small monthly fee. "People will line up to support it. You just need some computer types to help you out."

Wow. That was so tempting. By now it had occurred to me that I had completely miscalculated on the film's needs. It most certainly did not require my help in getting the word out. It was the audience who was left in need. So many people were so overcome by the experience, they were searching the web and finding my site after they saw the film. Many of them had no idea what they were looking for, they were just grasping around, and when they got to the site they knew what they were after: other people affected as deeply as them.

Initially, 90 percent of the discussion was about the film—what was happening up on the screen versus down in the audience. But there was a fascinating undercurrent about what it was doing to us. The film discussion died down eventually, and the personal stories edged their way to the forefront. The stories were so moving, the impact so powerful, that by February a member named Lydia suggested they should be gathered together in a book. Good God, I thought. A book is an enormous undertaking. It will never happen. But I told her she could give it a shot, see if she could recruit all the editors, proofreaders, artists, designers and an army of other volunteers prepared to pull this project together out of love. She did. She had a lot of help. Over the next year, more than 60 volunteers would labor to bring this book to the page. The selection committee read through more than 50,000 posts to choose the 178 pieces for this collection. A few stories were written specifically for this book, but the vast majority were just raw, immediate reactions posted directly on the website. Their authors never expected to find their words in print. We edited them a bit, tweaked a few here and there, but most of them appeared very close to the way you see them right now.

I'm deeply grateful to that volunteer team. They all have jobs and friends and family and lives of their own that they squeezed aside for the past year to bring this book into your hands. And I'm grateful to the authors for sharing their lives with us so candidly. They never expected to be authors. They were just people feeling pain or joy or heartbreak or redemption. People who refused to keep accepting that there are lies we have to tell. These are their stories. I hope you enjoy them as much as I did.

Dave Cullen
Founder of The Ultimate Brokeback Forum
http://DaveCullen.com/

1 James

—Jonathan Mortimer

It took me a long time to figure it out.

On December 12, 2005, I saw *Brokeback Mountain* at a crowded matinee in Manhattan with a close friend. The story, which I'd re-read for the first time since it appeared in *The New Yorker* in 1997, and the general air of expectancy around the film had made me eager to see it, but nothing could have prepared me for the impact of that first viewing. As my friend and I left the theatre, we exchanged no more than two or three sentences about the film, both of us feeling overwhelmed and stunned into silence.

When I returned home, I had to wait almost three weeks before the film opened in Sacramento, but already obsession had set in. I started reading the story almost daily, searched for whatever I could find online about *Brokeback Mountain*, found the Forum shortly after it began, and immersed myself in reading other people's comments, though making none of my own, because I couldn't understand why I was feeling the way I did.

I would see the film in the theater nineteen times. I would spend countless hours talking long distance with friends drawn in to the *Brokeback* phenomenon. But always, in the back of my mind, there was that lingering question: why was this happening to me? What was wrong with me?

Spring came. The film left the theatres, and the DVD came out. Even though the film had nowhere near the same emotional, quasi-physical impact on a television or computer screen, I still couldn't break free of it. When was this going to end?

Summer came. I happened to see a call for volunteer proofreaders in the Forum's Daily Sheet. I emailed the book project coordinator, and before I knew it, I had accepted the responsibility of being the senior editor of the book. Little did I know what I was in for!

By coincidence, if there is such a thing, one of our volunteers lives in South Africa. When I told her that I had once spent some time in her country, she asked which parts I had visited. In response, I sat down and started writing a short history of my stay there. And then the memories started flooding back.

I had gone to South Africa to visit a friend, Peter, whom I'd known since 1974, and who now lived in the Eastern Cape. Our original plan of touring round the Cape Province together didn't work out; instead, I went on to Cape Town alone.

On Saturday, March 1, 1980, I went with a friend of Peter's to a performance by Les Ballets Trockadero de Monte Carlo. Afterwards, we stopped by a pub off the beach in Sea Point for a couple of drinks. After closing time, we went for a walk along the Promenade and met some other friends, who joined us. One of the members of the other group and I started talking, and we soon fell behind the rest of the group. James and I spent the next three hours together, laughing, talking, walking hand-in-hand in the moonlight, both of us feeling the growing excitement of having found someone so special that, for the moment, nothing else mattered.

The time we spent together in the coming days was different from anything either had experienced before.

Between bouts of passionate lovemaking, James showed me some of his country. We spent a wonderful day touring the peninsula down to the Cape of Good Hope in his Morris Minor, visiting Cape Dutch estates, taking in the beauty of the landscape and the antics of baboons in heat. I was learning a great deal from him about the history and culture of the Western Cape and its people, and I started to see things through different eyes.

Some afternoons I would go and sit in the shop where he was working part-time, drinking Rooibos tea and listening to his talk. I was fascinated by his mind. I was completely happy just to be with him.

I had my visa extended—no easy task in those days—in order to stay in the country beyond my original departure date. In the end, we only had two-and-a-half weeks, but we made the most of every day.

We talked of our desire to be together always. However, when my departure became imminent, neither of us had the courage to make the decision. We were caught in a historical and political trap, and there didn't seem to be any way out of it. It was 1980, and apartheid was at its height; it would have been extremely difficult, if not impossible, for me to work there or for him to emigrate. I couldn't tell James that one word from him would make me stay, and he felt he couldn't ask me to give up my country for him.

The last night I was in Cape Town, we drove up to the top of Signal Hill overlooking the city. We sat drinking wine together as we watched the sun set. By this time, I was feeling something between depression and panic. It was like watching the sun set on my life. We went back to his house for our last night together and talked and wept for five or six hours.

James had arranged for me to stay with a couple of friends of his in Johannesburg for a few days before my return flight to America. Just before leaving for the airport, we said last good-byes on the phone. We could hardly speak. Later, I sat in the airport lounge with tears running down my cheeks, heartsick to be leaving him.

When I got back to the States, I went ahead with a previously-planned move to Atlanta. I wrote him several times, but his first letter to me wasn't mailed for a month, because it took me some time to get settled at a new address. Reading that first letter broke my heart. He had started it the day I left.

So it is done. I drove away quickly lest I should cry, and I thanked God for the boring work to occupy my mind. I left him on the pavement, and my life quite literally shattered. The end of the day came, and then the pain. Realization. I love him. I don't want to, but I love him as I've never loved before. He loves me for what I am: aging, cynical, even slightly evil, and altogether not very nice. But he loves me. Days—a postcard! Light. Despair. I love him, but I wish I didn't. I want him, I want him near. Unbearable night. Phone call! I hide my feelings, can't talk. Make conversation and an aching body—desire inspired by his voice—no—I love him! Good-bye. Days, ache, pain—on and on. Will it ever end? No.

So the rains came and the cold and the misery and ache. There was only me and tomorrow and tomorrow and tomorrow. Tomorrow is empty, and I'm alone as I've never been before. I love him. Oh God, if only I could kill it!

Early April: a letter. Flash of joy! Longing, fruitless desire, and the ever-present pain.

Next day: another letter! "The most natural reaction would, I suppose, be to 'seal off' that time in your life to avoid the sense of loss and futility involved in the circumstances." Yes, that's it: do that. "Seal off," try to forget. Put him right out of your life and mind.

More tomorrows, more loneliness, more pain. All the time, I feel a hand reaching out across the Atlantic, tugging, reminding. I can't forget. So write to the man. Words won't come. Can't think what to say. Rebellion. I feel like a man who knows he's dying of cancer. Days and more days. The dull ache of physical and mental longing never ceases.

And so a third letter.
Acceptance. I'll never get away from Jonathan Mortimer . . . .

I got a job, went about my business. I even found a new partner. But in spite of all that, I couldn't forget, and we continued to correspond.

Of course you are not wrong [James wrote]. Our relationship is far more than just physical contact, and somehow we managed to squeeze into such a short time far more than most people do in a lifetime. Of course we don't know each other in all our different facets, but I reckon I can read that soul of yours enough to make our relationship lasting.

However, James could not handle my new relationship, and a couple of years later he ended the correspondence. My partner and I started our own business and nearly worked ourselves to death, which no doubt contributed to the ending of that relationship in the late eighties. After that, I decided to make a clean break and left the country for a while to regroup.

In the spring of 1988, while I was staying with a friend just outside Barcelona, I came to see that I had really lost my way. I still hadn't found out who I was or arrived at a real adult sense of independence. And now what was I to do? I was forty-two years old, and I had no home, no job, no sense of direction.

I wrote to him. He called. He still loved me. "Come to South Africa. I'll take care of you." Those were probably the worst words he could have said to me at that moment. I couldn't let anyone take care of me. I had to learn to take care of myself.

Once again, we had failed to find a way to be together. This time it was my fault for sure. I couldn't bear the pain, and I did the only thing I could find to do about it. I unconsciously suppressed the memory, because I couldn't deal with it. It was hopeless. Forget it and get on with your life. I never wrote to him again.

So once again I came back to the States and started over. Eventually, I moved to California to go to graduate school. I did a good job of suppressing the memory: almost never did I let him seep into my conscious mind from that point on. Life got better, and I became more independent. But I paid a very steep price for that independence. I shut down emotionally and never could give myself to anyone else, not really.

Then along came *Brokeback Mountain*. Oh, the walls were very thick and strong that I had built around my memory of him.

But it all came back to me on the terrible weekend of September 9, 2006. It almost crushed me. I sat weeping uncontrollably for a man I had not seen in over twenty-six years. Surely he must be dead by now: the last time I talked with him, he was having heart trouble. But I had to know one way or the other. What *Brokeback* had finally made clear to me was that I had to deal with this now, or I would never be really alive again myself.

How could I find out? I wrote to an employer he used to work for, hoping someone could give me some information. Was he alive? If not, how and when did he die?

When I got up on September 12th (nine months to the day since I had first seen *Brokeback Mountain*), there was an email from the employer giving me his address and phone number—he was still in the very same house where we had been together all those years ago.

Minutes later, I was dialing his number. When he heard who was calling, he was so shocked that he dropped the phone. That first conversation lasted more than an hour, but I learned that he had never stopped loving me. He had also convinced himself that I was dead. He too had forced himself to forget it as best he could. There had never been anyone else, not really. He had poured himself into his work and had made a very successful career. But inside he was always alone, just like me. He told me that he has had a photograph of me on his bedside table for the last twenty-six years.

It turned out that our South African volunteer, Elle, lived just a short distance from his house. In the first couple of weeks after we reconnected, she first talked with him on the phone, then visited him in person. She took photos of him to send to me and gave him prints of photos I had sent of myself. Afterwards, she emailed me an account of her visit.

He welcomed me, both of us probably a bit nervous. I mean, there we were, total strangers, our only connection being that he met (and fell in love with) you twenty-six years ago, and I met you online about three weeks ago! But truly, he is such an easy man to talk to, very articulate, intelligent, very sure of himself in many ways, and such a gracious host.

It is very, very clear to me that he has always loved you deeply. When he lost track of you and presumed you dead, he gave up, buried you mentally and emotionally, and raised a tombstone in his heart to your memory. At the beginning of this year, after a bad health scare, he also gave up on himself—put his house in order, dug his grave, planned for his ending. He could see little left to live for and was making ready to go.

Then you called.

He says he now has a reason to carry on living. He tells me that friends are asking him, "What's happened? You look so different, so full of health." He has also become very emotional, which he says is not usual for him. I suspect he is going through a very natural grieving process for all the years you didn't have together and is maybe even fearing that the time that is left will be too short, too difficult.
What else can I tell you? He is lovely.

Since that first call, we have talked by phone every day. Finally, we have had the chance to work through some of the anger, the frustration, the hurt, the mistakes we had both made. We have been able to start to work through the things that went so wrong and get to know each other better. We have been falling in love all over again. Each of us still aches to hold the other in his arms. I will be going to Cape Town in November for a three-week visit, and we're going to try to work out a solution.

We haven't talked a lot about *Brokeback Mountain*, because it did not have quite the same impact on him as it did on me. Besides, I think it is something that I can explain much better when we are face-to-face. James has, however, begun to think of ours as "a Brokeback situation."

As the weeks have gone by, James's mood has changed. At first, he was wary, hesitant, inclined to dwell on obstacles. He has become increasingly relaxed, happier, less inclined to see only the difficulties.

James is now seventy, and I am sixty. I find that that doesn't make any difference.

James is the one great love of my life, and I am his. Had it not been for *Brokeback Mountain*, I would probably have gone to my grave without recovering this knowledge. How all this will play out remains uncertain, but one thing *is* certain, and that is that we gave ourselves to each other so completely, so definitively, so irrevocably that there is nothing either of us can ever do about that now. Some things, once done, can never be undone.

Jonathan Mortimer, 60, the senior editor of the Book Project, lives in Sacramento, California and works in state government. He posts under the name jlm1.

A cattle truck, running empty...

2 First Impressions

Many viewers were not prepared for what actually happened when they first watched Brokeback Mountain. *The selections below describe what some felt after their initial viewing.*

"Blowin' in the Wind"

—johnjay

When the movie ended, I just stayed in my seat through all the credits, giving time to compose myself before leaving. By the time I did get up and turn around, I was alone, as the others sitting behind me had already left; so no one saw how red my eyes were. The drive home started well. I had the radio off, since I wanted it quiet so I could mull over and replay different scenes in my mind without distraction.

After fifteen minutes or so, I had to stop doing that because there were just too many things getting to me. For some diversion, I turned the radio to an oldies station to which I frequently listen. They play songs of the 1960s, which was when I grew up, and those songs usually remind me of simpler times in my life.

When I turned on the radio, Peter, Paul, and Mary's version of "Blowin' in the Wind" was playing. It's a song I grew up with, one I've heard hundreds of times. I thought, "Good, I like them; this'll calm me down." Just as I thought that, I immediately felt uneasy as words I've known for most of my life started to sink in with new meaning. "How many years must a mountain exist/Before it is washed to the sea?/How many years can some people exist/Before they're allowed to be free?/How many times can a man turn his head/And pretend that he just doesn't see?"

I involuntarily started to feel tears welling up. Then a few sobs. Then on the radio, "How many deaths will it take till he knows/That too many people have died?" As soon as I heard that last bit with their haunting harmony, I totally lost it. Many thoughts flooded through me: thoughts about the scene of Jack's murder, thoughts of that Wyoming fence where Matthew Shepard was killed and where that ubiquitous portrait of him hung, and thoughts of a friend who died fifteen years ago of AIDS. I started crying uncontrollably and quickly had to pull off and stop on the shoulder of the road. I turned off the radio and just leaned against the steering wheel crying so hard. After a few minutes, the crying subsided, and I felt calm and okay and continued home in a sort of post-cathartic peace. I imagine in future days and weeks, little things in life—things I have been totally used to—will unexpectedly hit me in a new light and remind me of them.

My Folks Finally Understand

—Ted Fry

My folks, both just under eighty, responded to my gentle harangue and saw *Brokeback* today in Lancaster, Pennsylvania, the Pennsylvania Dutch country. Getting around isn't easy for them; they're at the age where they bought a new house "so they could be all on one floor." They restrict their travel to absolute necessities. They haven't made the seventy-mile trip here to Philadelphia in almost fifteen years.

They're tremendously decent, salt-of-the-earth people, despite a general outlook that makes them typical of the deep red state region in which they live. They've intellectually accepted who I am since my late teens (thirty years), but there's always been an unfathomable emptiness in our relationship. I've never been able to get beyond their old-world morality and completely communicate to them what it means to be [something], and to need something, that contradicts such a fundamental part of their conventions.

They're very well-read and can appreciate anything well-made, so I restricted my sales pitch to the film's artistic merits. I likened it to older films to set the mood for them, like *Hud*, or *The Last Picture Show*, but I prayed they'd both understand why it was so important to me that they go.

My mother dutifully e-mailed immediately upon their return from the showing, "Don thought it was worth breaking his thirty-year theater boycott. Wish I could be there to give you a hug. Beautiful picture."

My folks are Ennisean in their economy of words and stingier yet with their feelings. For them to send me the foregoing is just huge.

I sat down, put the soundtrack on, and collapsed into the kind of cathartic bawling I haven't experienced since I was a kid. My folks finally understand something of my life.

Ted Fry, 46, currently lives in Philadelphia, Pennsylvania, and is employed as a financial manager. He posts under the screen name PennQuaker.

Hit Me Like a Missile

— BenKing

It hit me like a missile. I had no idea this movie would do that. The day after my boyfriend and I first saw it, I had to go away for a week on business. Thinking about the movie made me miss my boyfriend so much. In my spare time on the road, I was on the internet the whole time trying to figure out if there was a way we could obtain a marriage license. I was calling my boyfriend every minute I could to tell him how much I loved him, how the last four years with him had been the best time I'd ever had, and how, as soon as we could, we needed to bring together all of our family, friends—whomever really mattered to us—and avow our love for one another.

Depth Charge

—Jim McNulty

I'm Scottish and live in Spain, and I have just come, virgin-like, to *Brokeback*. It has dropped a depth charge into my very existence, blowing away all the digressionary rubbish fifty years on the planet have filled my brain with, reminding me, perhaps just in time, that love in all its forms is the only imperative to which the soul should lean.

I hope I can take the powerful emotions this film has evoked in me into the rest of my life!

Ang and the gang, you should be very proud! This is a life-changing work of art!

Jim McNulty, 50, works in Spain as a property developer. He posts under the screen name Jimspain.

Flowers

—Changedforever

I'm in my mid-forties, a straight woman in a long happy marriage who has been extremely fortunate, but this film has spoken to me in a way I've yet to fully understand. I've seen it three times and have been devastated every time. The best analogy I can come up with is it's like being sucked through a wormhole and re-materialized on the other side pretty much the same as before, but with the molecules in different places. I'm me, but I'm different. This film has changed me, and it's changed me for the better. I hope I'm more tolerant, more forgiving, and more willing to live for today because today is really all we have.

The morning after the first time I saw this film, I went out and bought a small bunch of yellow freesias and roses—yellow for faithfulness, freesias because they bloom for only a short time, but are so wonderful, and roses for love. As I put them in the vase, I turned to my husband and said, "They're for Jack and Ennis." He didn't laugh. He nodded and kissed me.

Changedforever, 44, is a journalist and editor who is married with a teenage son at university.

A Huge Punch of Emotion

—kaboyz

I don't recall having a desire to go run out and see *Brokeback Mountain*. I think I assumed it would be all gay-bashing, and who would want to see that? Plus, I didn't want my heart to get broken.

My boyfriend Marc wanted to see it, so I agreed; we went, but it was sold out. I was a bit relieved because I was beginning to realize that from what I was hearing about this movie that it was going to kick my ass. After seeing it, I was in shock. It was such a huge punch of emotion that I couldn't identify one appropriate emotion to let out. I cried myself to sleep that night, the first time I could remember crying in over six years.

I felt emotionally awakened. I guess that prior to *Brokeback*, I avoided my emotions, tried to stay stress-free; and, in doing so, became a laid-back, unaffected kind of guy. Deep down, though, I was searching for my soul, trying to figure out who I was and why I was so frequently sad and depressed.

Then I saw *Brokeback Mountain*, and all that changed. I related so much to the story that it made me realize I had deep-rooted, unidentified emotions associated with my sexuality that were now very clear to me. I don't know if I would have ever discovered all of this without *Brokeback Mountain*.

I am still in love with the story, and I now appreciate my life, my friends, and my boyfriend so much more. I now have this drive to make only the best of things. *Brokeback Mountain* turned on the emotions inside me that had been shut down for way too long.

This author is a 27-year-old man from Hauppauge, New York.

Numbness

—Tobysgirl

Are we so powerfully affected by this movie because so much of our lives are numb? And this movie won't let us be numb?

Settling for Crumbs

—SYC

I was stunned. I sat in the theater after everyone left and cried.

I'm a lesbian and struggling to find happiness in life. I have issues to resolve with a special lady in my life. I have some individuals in my past who linger in my memories as a disappointment. Of course, there are also straight women around me today who cannot return my affections, even if some of them, in another world, would feel safe to explore that side of themselves.

So the movie hit home for me: the concepts of lost love, of yearning, of regret, of impossible circumstances, of waiting, of hoping, of settling for crumbs of love when you are capable of giving so much more.

I loved the undertones in the movie: the concept of masculinity and success by which Jack's father-in-law judges him, and the theme of the role of family in our lives. There is also a lesson about not just finding a partner, but finding out what is important in your life and fighting for that—something Ennis failed to do, and not just with Jack.

I loved the movie for what it was on its face, a great film about two guys who are forever bound to each other in the face of a society which forbids their love.

Ripped Down Every Wall

—Jack Schilling

It has made me think, reach out, contact the love of my life, [and] consider geographic moves; in short, it ripped down every wall I'd built around my heart.

Jack Schilling, 51, is a horticulturist/garden designer who lives in Denver, Colorado. His screen name is brokeback_1.

Twilight Zone

—Nicole

I dragged my rather conservative hubby to see *Brokeback Mountain*. I warned him not to make comments or anything during the film, because I just knew he would either snort or mumble something like, "Oh, gawd!" during the love scenes. He actually behaved pretty well.

Anyway, the movie ends, and I'm crying like a baby, and he turns to me and says:

Hubby: (*frowning*) They shouldn't make movies like this.

Me: (*Uh-oh, here we go. I don't need this right now.*) What do you mean? (*Sniff!*)

Hubby: The ending was so sad. I don't like feeling like crap after a movie.

Me: Oh, honey! (*Floodgate opens*)

Hubby: What?

Me: (*self-conscious*) Am I the only person crying in the theater?

Hubby: No. There are a couple of guys crying over there, and that girl . . . and *I* even had to hold back tears.

He told me in the car that they should have ended up together eventually on a ranch somewhere—I thought I had entered the twilight zone at that point!

So, [the] big, macho, conservative, sports-loving, Stallone fan actually loved the movie. He's so getting lucky tonight …

Nicole is a 31-year-old woman from Florida.

Opposite of a Horror Movie

—Jean Aubé

I felt like I was seeing a movie for the very first time. *Brokeback Mountain* is the opposite of a horror movie: instead of locking our doors afterwards, we leave them wide open.

Jean Aubé, 56, is a freelance graphic designer and illustrator who resides in Montréal, Québec, Canada. His screen name is john john.

3 The Moon's Reflection

—Michael O'Neill

I am sixty-two.

No man who is gay does not live in the closet, betraying the truth about himself, denying who he is by presenting himself as who he is not, often many times a day — in the bank, at the laundry, at the gas station, to a neighbor, to a stranger — not just for convenience, but out of fear, mistrust, anxiety that is a low-grade constant, because no gay man has not seen the hostility, not encountered the contempt at one time or another. Few have not felt personally threatened; many have felt the smashing blows. Every gay man at one time knows the toll this disdain or derision takes, but if it is sometimes dealt with ably, too often it is not.

As Ennis says in the movie, "You ever get the feelin', I don't know, when you're in town, and someone looks at you, suspicious. . .like he knows." Gay people ache at seeing the harm that self-loathing exacts in the deception and fear brought into the lives of two nineteen-year-old high-school dropouts, bewildered at what unfolds in them, in their world, in 1963, in Riverton, Wyoming. All gay men know the heartache of these two protagonists as intimately as their own, in their own loves and friendships lost. *Brokeback Mountain* is about their lives. It is mine.

I grew up Catholic in a small town in Arizona, where shame was as wide and deep as that Wyoming sky in *Brokeback*. I felt something was very wrong with me. I could tell nobody about it, because I didn't know why or how it had formed itself in me, where it got its name, how it found me, when it arrived, how it sprang forth. Even as a young boy, I was attracted to males, with the raw sexual fantasies children know to keep secret. I was thrilled by male nakedness. I would linger in the area where men undressed to go swimming and found myself going back there innumerable times while we were at the pool.

I started having sex shortly after puberty, at age thirteen, usually with friends, classmates in the usual genre of boys' circles. I knew something was terribly wrong with me when a little later a high school counselor told me it was a "character defect," a kind of mental aberration. I was happy to know it had another name, a name taking precedence over "queer" and "fag." I knew I was devious, sneaky, a liar, fundamentally defective because my furtive encounters were kept secret, tracks covered. I knew, above all, I should never say I was queer.

At age fifteen, I fell in love with a boy who was one year younger. He was thin, a taller boy, very handsome, very sweet. He loved me intensely. I was athletic, muscled, very macho, or so I tried hard to appear. He was a very sad kid who had been in foster homes throughout all his grade-school years, a series of homes where the fathers or the older sons of the pious foster families or other, older foster kids would regularly molest him.

My friend Billy wanted to be around me all the time, and whenever we were safely alone he would kiss me and hold me in his arms and tell me how much he loved me. I did not want him to kiss me on the lips. I did not return his kisses. Like Ennis in *Brokeback Mountain*, I would tell him I wasn't queer, that I had a character defect that let me have sex with him, but that two guys couldn't love each other because it was against natural law, that he only thought he loved me, but was mistaken, a kind of mental aberration: it was a sin. Yet there was not only the turbulence of a troubled love affair; there was more than just sin. We would go dove hunting and take long hikes into the surrounding hills and mountain-climb or swim in the river, camp out at the lake over weekends, sneak into the movies, and all the other exhilarating boyish adventures being together allowed.

And I was glad as day for his company, even as my increasingly deliberate lack of response hurt him deeply. He often would cry or not talk, becoming sullen and withdrawn. I was scared. I became afraid that people would soon see or hear something, and I told him I didn't want him touching me in public, even if he thought people were not around.

We often slept over at each other's houses; both our families liked us. One night, after a late movie, he came to my house to sleep over. We were having sex in my bed, as we often did. My dad got up for some other reason; maybe we were making noise. He came in to check and switched the light on. Billy and I were entwined naked, and we froze for the longest instant. Then my dad switched the light off and closed the door.

The next morning I was terrified to go to breakfast, but he called us. We crept into the kitchen with hideous foreboding. My dad said not one word about what he had seen but was in fact very friendly. He made pancakes for us.

A few years later when I wrote my dad that I was a homosexual, he told me not to worry, many people go through similar phases. Even then he never mentioned the night he turned the light on. Perhaps that early view prepared him for what my mother would find herself to be so traumatically unprepared. For years, she would send me newspaper clippings of one person or another who had left the "gay lifestyle" to become heterosexual, of one psychiatrist or another who had devised a cure, of some priest in Chicago or Denver whose methods had turned gays around.

I was becoming afraid that Billy's neediness would arouse suspicions and expose what I had so tautly kept hidden. I finally told him I didn't want to spend time with him anymore because he was, in Catholic terms, "a near occasion of sin." For several weeks or months, I made him miserable by refusing to see him. He would come to the house on the pretext of visiting others in my family, but I would ignore him. Once I found him on the street outside my high school as if he had chanced by. I refused to even acknowledge him. He followed me for blocks before I told him to go away, not to visit me, not to call me, not to write me. After a few minutes I relented, but it changed our friendship.

We went back to spending a lot of time together that summer and into the fall working for the campaign of John Kennedy for president. In my senior year, I was given a scholarship to a private boarding school, and I was thrilled to leave home, in no small part because it would separate us finally. Yet he came up to visit me several times that fall, hitchhiking or getting his mom to drive him. He seemed to grow sadder and withdrawn. I would see him on those weekends I came home and over the Christmas holidays, often again staying over at each other's houses, still committing sin, mortal sin. He had started seeing an older married man in his twenties whom he liked. The man had been a driver in the Kennedy campaign and had two small kids.

I was glad to hear it, as I thought it would relieve me of the burden of guilt and responsibility for his emotional and sexual neediness. After the Christmas break, I intentionally began staying at school most weekends, going places with new friends and classmates. I saw a lot less of Billy.

One Thursday evening in spring, my mom called to tell me Billy had shot himself in the mouth and was dead.

He has haunted my life. I told his mother about our relationship, because I felt I had to confess my part: I had to tell her my part in driving him to despair. She thought that was small potatoes, had already known about it, but she suffered terribly the unrelieved self-recrimination of his loss, blaming herself for his tragic death, nearly wild with intolerable sorrow. She drank a lot. We spent much time together over that summer, nearly every day. Then I moved to New York, never to live in Arizona again. Billy's mom moved to Tacoma, finished high school and college, became a high school counselor, and adopted two teenage girls, sisters.

In death he became my constant companion, whom in life I had tried to flee. I still carry him around with me daily, though I have almost never talked about it in forty-five years. I still see him as a boy, head tilted, smile slight and abashed, his dark hair, thin face. I recall his face at odd times in any day, and we have talked often through the years in my dreams. I love his visiting me in my dreams, even in a recurring dream of unalleviated sadness that over the years has grown less frequent, where he appears not talking, with no skin, his raw naked body wet from tears. In this dream there is only sobbing, but in most dreams we talk of many things. When Jack said to Ennis, "I wish I knew how to quit you," its resonance hit sharply, its torn, bare cry piercing and true.

Brokeback Mountain reverberates in my life. I am profoundly shaken over the memories it gave life to in Ennis and Jack, memories I thought had been shielded and well-insulated long ago. Memories of two sad, poor boys I've mourned all these years: one who lost his life, one who lost his love.

Brokeback Mountain knew somehow what I carry in my heart; it guessed the ghost kept pastured away in a concealed, secluded valley, its howls at night over the distance heard below a small moon mainly in sleep. Sorrow's pure springs are each unique, yet all the same, no matter their names.

Michael O'Neill has lived with his partner, Tom Leo, in Eastern Long Island for thirty-nine years, where he serves as an immigrant rights activist. He posts under the screen name Sagha/Mo.

4 Family Values

—Tory Kennedy

I have a rather uplifting story for all of you in the closet. Oddly enough, it begins with the horrifying events at the Oscars. I was so unbearably depressed about that awful night and couldn't imagine how something so terrible could have happened. Anyway, the next day I came home from school early, and my older brother was home because of spring break. He asked me what I thought of the Oscars, and I admitted I had hated it. I wasn't "out" to him technically, but I always felt it was the proverbial elephant in the room. I knew he knew; we just never talked about it. He continued to prod me as to why I had hated it and what award it was that upset me so much, and finally, I said it—I had seen *Brokeback Mountain*.

He didn't believe me, so I showed him my movie ticket stubs that I had saved. Then he asked why I hadn't told him I'd seen it, why I had lied about it so many times before. I said, "Because then I would have had to tell you I am gay." Wow, he was so shocked! I couldn't believe it! I would've bet a million dollars that he knew beyond a shadow of a doubt. Not only have I lived with the guy for nineteen years, but also, he really is my best friend; he knows me so well, yet this—he was completely thrown for a loop. He was terrified at first, only because he had never expected such a thing. After the initial onset of shock had worn off, though, he began asking me questions: "How long have I known?" and "What is it that I like about guys?" Stuff like that.

Then he began to get interested in gay rights and homosexuals portrayed in the media. He asked me about gay marriage, adoption, and *Queer as Folk*. We talked for two hours. He invited me to hang out with him and his friends that night, something he rarely does; he said he felt we should bond. He wanted the first time I came out to be memorable. He invited me to watch *Transamerica* with him. Later on, I found out that when he talked about it with his girlfriend, he started crying because he felt so bad for me. He understood how hard it was for gays, especially in such a conservative state as Virginia. He had never really thought about it personally. He couldn't bear to think how hard it must be to keep it in for so long. He said he could easily put aside any discomfort he might have in discussing men with me, knowing how uncomfortable it must be for me every day in the straight world.

He said he got mad at his friend for using the word "faggot," and he has vowed to ram all cars with the bumper sticker "Marriage = Man & Woman." I'm amazed at how much this seems to have affected him. He seems to be analyzing many things from a homosexual perspective. He even watched the gay channel Logo the other day, all by himself, and the program was about a transvestite! I knew he would accept my homosexuality, but I had no idea he would take such a sudden, active role about it. He said he felt like my coming out has made us closer. It is doubly nice that I have come out not only about being gay, but also about my love for *Brokeback Mountain*, since it had kind of been my catalyst for the whole event anyway.

We talked about the movie and what effects I felt it has had for both society and me. We talked about certain elements and themes in it. He has agreed to read the short story later this week, and I'll find out how he thinks Jack was killed. It's really an amazing feeling to finally be able to talk about something that has been such a huge part of my life for so long with my best friend and brother. All my life I'd kept it a secret, even though I identified a huge chunk of my selfhood in terms of my sexuality. So to finally talk with him about it and be tackled with nothing but love and acceptance is a wonderful, wonderful feeling. I only wish all homosexuals had the warm welcome from their friends and family that I was fortunate enough to experience.

A few weeks later Tory came out to his sister.

About a month ago, I posted about coming out to my brother. He took it enormously well, crying for me and becoming actively aware of the gay community. A few days ago, I came out to my younger sister. She was shocked and couldn't think of anything to say except that she loved me. I knew she would accept it; my whole family is liberal. I talked with her about it a little bit over the next couple of days, but that was pretty much it. I didn't think it was anything particularly significant for her.

That's what I thought until an hour ago when she gave me a poem she had written for me. I was floored when I read this and that my fifteen-year-old baby sister would write this just because she wanted to do so. I found it very touching. She's not even an English-type person; she hates reading.

> Digging for the answers,
> Been digging for so long.
> His fingers red and raw
> Bleeding for hours,
> But he keeps digging
> To satisfy the need,
> The hunger he feels.
> Trying to find the answers.
> Find his identity.
> Finally he does,
> And he is silenced.
> He found who he is,
> But is afraid to expose himself.
> He is bound to the silence,
> A prisoner.
> So he buries himself in the hole.
> Wait for the perfect time,
> Time to broadcast
> Tell all
> And unveil who he is.

This really touched me. I don't know where she got it. I never mentioned anything about "finding my identity" or "burying myself," but it really made me think she gets it. She's not gay, but she understands what I'm going through. My brother did that, too, for me, in a different way.

We're not a very sensitive, emotional type of family. We very rarely say that we love each other. In fact, my sister was too shy even to be in the room when I read it [her poem]; she made me wait till she left. Somehow, though, both of my siblings have managed to show their deep love and understanding for me. It absolutely blows my mind. I am intrigued now to see how my parents will react. I don't see how they could top the last two.

Tory Kennedy is a 19-year-old electrical engineering student from Fredericksburg, Virginia. He uses Tory Kennedy *as his screen name.*

No suitcase, just a grocery sack...

5 Aftershocks

Later, Forum members described what happened the next day and in the days that followed.

Now What?

—lltra2005

Of course I'd been hearing a lot about *Brokeback*. My wife wanted to go. I really didn't have any interest. Not because I am homophobic, but I am just not a love-story kind of guy; give me a good psychological thriller. Nonetheless, I went like a good husband.

Since I have seen it, I am not feeling like a good husband.

Wow! I had no idea what kind of effect this movie would have on me. It has consumed my every waking thought and has even wakened me out of sleep. I am confused, depressed, anxious, and not really sure how to deal with it yet. I fear it is an awakening . . . and that scares me.

The confusion comes from feelings about which I am not sure. The first love scene just seemed more an act of desperation than love or emotion. However, at each encounter after that, I found myself silently cheering the guys on, wanting to see them embrace, hug, [or] kiss—not for the sexuality, but for the emotions of their love and passion. I cried, especially during the scene when they met for the first time after four years, and they kissed outside Ennis's apartment. All the while, I am trying to not show my wife (sitting next to me) any emotion at all for fear she would ask about my reaction. By the end of the movie, I felt strong emotions for both Ennis and Jack—not just the obvious sadness and feelings of loneliness, but sympathy and empathy. Ever since I left the theater, I feel the need to find a guy and hug and cry with him.

I am not sure if what I am feeling is overwhelming sympathy for two people in forbidden love, or if this story helped to open a side to me I didn't know was there—the need for male companionship. I've felt drawn to men in the past, but I just figured that it was like being attracted to any personality that meshes with your own. Now I am not so sure it has been all that simple.

Much like Ennis, I can't open up to my wife. I really don't think she would understand, and that would only make me feel worse. I've been married thirteen years with two kids and love them all very much, but now what?

Chipped at the Edges

—Evie

This movie does break open something in each of us, gay or not. I am most positively straight, married with two kids. I still can't figure out what hold it has on me. I almost feel it brought on a sort of midlife crisis—a realization that my life is probably the best that it will ever be, that the days when all possibilities were open to me are far in my past; that love will never again be as passionate and as all-consuming as it was in my youth; a strong feeling of myself marching into deep middle age without a whole lot to show for myself.

Maybe for each of us *Brokeback* magnifies whatever inadequacy or discontent we feel. I can't say I am alone in life, but do I have an Ennis/Jack connection with anyone? Not really.

I have often wondered this: does *Brokeback* have the same power over people who are living lives they consider happy and rich and fulfilling, or is it just we who are a little chipped at the edges who suffer so?

Body, Mind, and Soul

—magicmountain

You walk into the cinema with your chocolate-topped ice cream, expecting to be entertained by an interesting film. Instead, you sit there and find yourself being kicked in the guts, shot through the heart, and clobbered about the head at the same time. You stagger out of the cinema in a daze. You stay in this condition for weeks on end:

- You become disinterested in everything that used to engage your interest.
- You go off your food. It is hard to sleep.
- You feel totally shaken up on all levels: body, emotions, mind, and soul.
- You are filled with grief and longing, which maddens you because you don't know where to put these feelings or what to do with them.
- It's like being in love-hopelessly in love with someone or something out of reach.
- You go back repeatedly to see the film in order to gain some peace, but the next morning you wake up with the same ache. Are you going mad?

Some process is at work inside, and you have no choice but to surrender to it and let it work its way through your system at its own pace to some purpose you don't yet understand.

You often find yourself moving into a meditative state. You join this Forum, which becomes like a daily journal keeping you sane and helping along the process that is occurring within you as you take on board the meditations of others from so many perspectives. It is like a giant thought-and-feeling bubble which we share to help each other along.

It feels like great energy is surging through you at all levels:

- At the corporal level: There is a stirring of libido at the erotic power of this love story. Eros is a powerful force.
- At the emotional level: There is much crying and grief for Ennis and Jack, ourselves, and our remembered pain.
- At the cognitive level: There is intense analysis of the characters in a desire to understand their motivations and the meaning of symbols in this complex and multi-layered film. How far are we Ennis and Jack? Are these characters and the world they inhabit a representation of elements in a single mind—our mind?
- At the spiritual level: This film speaks directly to the innermost part of us, and this is what gives *Brokeback* its almost hypnotic power. It is trying to tell us

things that normally come to us in flashes when we are in deep grief or high emotion or in our dreams. Some have likened this experience to the response to great tragedy: pity, terror, and the cleansing catharsis of feelings.

There is a great urgency to understand what is being communicated and to respond. This film and its aftermath are turning us into poets, psychologists, and philosophers.

All this because of a "film about gay cowboys . . . ."

A 58-year-old resident of Sydney, Australia, magicmountain is a counselor, writer and editor who shares her life with her husband and their poodle.

I Don't Want to Get Over It

—danac

Since my obsession began, I've been told to "grow up," "get over it," and "shut up about it." But I don't want to get over it. I love the fact that this film made me sad. I love that it stirred up feelings I haven't felt in a long time. I love the fact that I can still be moved to tears by love and by passion, not just by tragedy.

I love that I want to put my hand on the face of every gay man or woman who feels less than [sic] and say, "It's all right."

I love asking people who feel threatened by two men loving each other what they are really afraid of. No one ever has an answer.

I love that a part of me is permanently hurt by homophobia. I'm happy to wear a "notch" scratched on my face because so many people are sad.
The metaphor of the lasso moves me because not only does it signify how Ennis became tangled up in Jack and that Jack roped him for life, but also because it means to me that, as human beings and souls, we are all tangled up in each other; and The Maker will one day question why we did not love more.

Dana, 58, who lives with her husband in New York City, is also a painter, cook and property investor. Danac is the screen name she uses.

Erased Horizon

—bluehorse

Why do some people walk out of the movie and go to dinner and talk about the weather while others walk out of the theater to find the horizon has been erased?

Bluehorse is 40 years old and lives in San Francisco, and prefers to remain anonymous at this time..

Freak Factor

—MarriedMan

Prior to *Brokeback's* release last winter, I was prepared for it, but foolishly put off seeing it in the theater out of the fear of having to explain why I was going to see it. Yes, I'm a guy who's married with kids. I took the book out of the library and read the short story. I watched it once and enjoyed it. Then I watched it again. And again. I must have watched it seven or eight times so far. I've slo-mo'ed all the great scenes and replayed some of the others, too. I've analyzed and obsessed so much over this film in the last month that it's hard to explain.

My wife and I have been going through a rough time, so I was seriously upset about that; and the raw emotion in the film affected me, too. She watched it, but generally referred to it as the "fag" movie. She still is unaware how incredibly hard this film has hit me. I've always found film to be an escape hatch, but the only way I can explain its profound effect on me over the last month is that I can identify with so much of the hardship displayed in so many ways in the story; and I see so much of myself in Ennis. Knowing that there are other straight people who understand and empathize with that helps alleviate the "freak factor," as someone else described it, for me.

MarriedMan is a 51-year-old community planner from Orange County, New York who is very involved in community preservation efforts.

Doing A Lot of Crying

—BrokenOkie

I live in the general region of Childress—where the movie was banned—and well remember the gay bashings/murders that were not uncommon around here during the late seventies/early eighties and even still. A friend of mine (who, for a while, was much more than that) was one of many innocent victims. The attack on him was similar to Jack's. He was dragged out to a remote area, then stabbed and left to drown in his own blood; his body not found for days.

I can't begin to imagine the impact this movie has had, and will continue to have, in my life. Right now, all I know for sure is that I can't get it out of my mind. When I think of the scenes in the tent and the summer the guys spent together, I cry with joy. When I think of the separation Ennis and Jack endured all those years, I cry for their heartbreak. When I think of Ennis being all alone in that trailer with only the shirts as a "physical" part of Jack, I cry. When I think of Jack's little boy growing up without his dad (and likely having to always endure the story of how he died), I cry. Doing a lot of crying, it seems. This too shall pass, when the time is right.

Glenn, a self-employed accountant, is 49 and lives in Oklahoma.

Spiritual Hunger

—Cowboy Dave

First time: saw it with pardner G, and another gay couple. I had to keep a lid on the flood inside because it would have been really too much. At the end, I just corked all this so I could function socially. Our gay pals had misty eyes. Mine were dry because letting it out would have been a lot more than a tear in the corner of my eye. I faltered a couple times walking away from the theater, but the strength of it was scary enough to let me force it back in the bottle.

Next two times were alone, and what a relief. G was out of town. I'm the one who was married with kids, so I have a lot of history that he doesn't have; and there were parts of this movie I needed to go over with just myself. The second time, I cried comfortably by myself. When it was over, I had this huge spiritual hunger and peace. I drove out to the Navajo Reservation, Big Sky country, for a couple hours. Everything felt so real. It was beautiful.

This last time, I had the same feeling of peace and clarity, but had to go straight home. I feel like I'm getting somewhere, but I don't know where. I'm at a place in my life where more than I dared hope for has really worked out, but I don't know what's next. This movie is showing me that, first off, I don't really know what just happened either. Perhaps I need to see this more fully before I can see what's next.

Is That So Much to Ask?

—Jermaine Peters

I've just turned twenty and live in Australia.

I don't feel I fit into any category or stereotype. My feeling is that the stereotype hurts gay people a lot—the sort of "if you're gay, you should act like this" thing—and that really gets me. Being gay is not a choice or conscious decision. I knew from a young age that I was attracted to boys, and saw girls mainly as friends and people with whom to talk.

I'm partly in the closet; I came out to my mum a year ago. It took a lot of courage to do that. I remember saying to Mum, "You know, I never wanted to tell you because I thought you'd stop loving me." While they can tell you mothers love you unconditionally, you never want to test that. She said that she accepted me being gay and loved me no matter what.

So far, I have to admit that, despite living in a small regional town, I have been fairly shielded. Some people refuse to serve me; I get called "faggot" occasionally. I can sort of shrug it off, but I wonder how these people can do that. They don't realize how much it hurts and that they're hurting another human being.

Brokeback Mountain has been so powerful for me. It was the first time in my life I had seen a true connection between two men—no stereotypes, no big drama scenes, just two men having a deep emotional connection. It sort of gave me hope, in spite of the fact that my feeling at the end of the movie was that for the rest of his life Ennis may never move on past Jack.

The second thing that really made me react so strongly to the movie and affected me deeply was that Jack and Ennis were kept apart by society and society's views. It hit home for me because I thought that's probably what is going to keep me from having a relationship too. I've never had a boyfriend, and the film makes me think that this is the way my life might be. I may eventually find someone, but we will be kept apart by society. That hurts, really deep down. I dream of having a husband/life partner/whatever-the-heck-we-need-to-call-them in the future and having a normal life where we both work, take holidays together, and sit and talk. Is that so much to ask?

It seems that for our society it is. That's what really hit home for me in *Brokeback Mountain*; it was sort of a "this is how your life may turn out." I don't want it to be like that, but I feel doomed.

Jermaine Peters is 20 years old, and a retail supervisor/administration manager from New South Wales, Australia. He posts under the screen name Jermaine P.

Denied

–Paul Wheelock

The dire emotions I felt after the Academy Award debacle was a magnified version of what I felt about the movie. Life imitates art. Once again denied. Denied who I am. Denied whom I love. Denied how I live. Denied my art. It was not like this was a marginal movie that might win the Academy Award if luck was with it. It was (is) the best, no question; but denied, denied, denied. I am so sick of being denied. Look at what happened to Jack because Ennis denied him. Heartache and destruction everywhere, self-destruction and so much collateral destruction—including the audience. The Academy perfectly perpetuates the experience of the movie: "You cannot have your love, your marriage, your life, your art."

Paul Wheelock (54) is a single college professor from Syracuse, New York. He posts under the name of 1224butternut.

Brokeback Fever I

—Wayne Courtois

I think Ang Lee should get his ass over here and clean my house. It's not my fault that I can't concentrate or get anything done!

Wayne Courtois is 52 years old and the author of two novels. He lives in Kansas, Missouri with his partner of eighteen years. His screen mame is waynerman.

Brokeback Fever II

—kumari

And after he's done at your house, he needs to come and help my kids with their homework. The teachers at school are probably thinking I'm out of town and my husband has been in charge.

Kumari is a 33-year-old data analyst and resident of Baltimore, Maryland, She is married with two children.

Utter Gayness

—Michael Perkins

Tonight, I went to my fifth viewing of *Brokeback Mountain*. My one and only goal was to enjoy the complete, utter gayness of the story, and it did not disappoint. Sad, depressing, uplifting, tender, erotic, painful, and depressing. I love this story and these characters.

Michael Perkins is 45 and is the father of three daughters. He lives in the Midwest and works as a corporate trainer . He psosts under the screen name mwp2paris.

I Am Ennis

—Mike80

The truth is, I am Ennis.

I thought I'd come to terms with my "gayness" long ago—when I was fifteen or so. But now I realize that I was so damn wrong. It was as if I said to myself, "Okay, man, you're gay. So what? Forget about it. There are lots more important things here you have to do."

The truth is, I'm twenty-five now, and I'm still not out. The past ten years, I've been living in my own trailer with my soul sealed and my true nature and my identity buried somewhere deep inside so that even I wouldn't have to face it. Maybe it is because I'm really very much like Ennis. I'm an introverted guy who has some trouble with expressing his feelings and emotions—though I usually smile and laugh much more than Ennis and definitely speak a lot more. Maybe it's because living in the 2000s in a small town in Russia doesn't differ much from living in 1960s Wyoming. Maybe it's both.

The truth is, all those years I've been living with stereotypes about gay people. What nonsense, huh?—a gay with stereotypes about gay people. I thought the only way for me to accept, to come to terms with myself would be entering the gay subculture. I wouldn't say that it disgusted me or that I didn't like it, but I just felt, and feel now, that gay life was not for me. I thought the only thing all gay men were looking for was a fuck-and-good-bye. Oh Lord, now I see how I was wrong! I've been living with self-denial, even self-hatred sometimes.

After *Brokeback*, I think I really started coming to terms with who I am and what I want in my life. I'm not a "gay/queer/homo" (in the stereotyped sense of those words). I'm just a man who desperately seeks another man to love and to be loved by. In *Brokeback Mountain*, the Ennis inside me saw what awaits him if he lives his life the way he was living all these years, and he got scared to death.

However, here comes another problem: I looked out of my trailer, but all I saw was a desert. Now I know what I want and what I need so desperately, but I don't know where to go or what to do with all this. After watching/reading "Brokeback Mountain" so many times, all Ennis's pain and loneliness have seeped into my soul; it is my pain and my loneliness now. My heart aches. I've totally fallen apart and can't recover my integrity. My soul is torn. It's not something whole now, but half of a soul longing for its other half.

It might sound crazy or selfish, but I envy Ennis so much because he had his Jack; he had his Brokeback. And Lord, I'm sure now that it's better to have my Brokeback, at least for a little while, or even only to have had that drowsy embrace (oh God, I can barely see the keyboard because of tears) than living all my life without even taking a chance to find the way to my Brokeback. Then I may live the rest of my life totally ruined and heartbroken, but I would have those sweet memories to warm up my lonely days a little.

Shit, Jack fuckin' Twist, where are you? I swear I would open up to your love and give you all my love. I would hold on to you and never let go. I would never fail you.

Self-Discovery

—Titus

As a minister and a former student of psychology, I can't help but draw parallels between what I've been feeling and the grieving process I see all around me in my work. What I have experienced is a condensed version of what we go through when we lose someone we love.

When I first saw the movie, I was relieved that it hadn't been a tear-jerker after all. It was brilliant and lovely, but not personally painful. Yet over the next twenty-four hours, I felt increasingly numb; I'd been in a kind of shock at what I had seen onscreen and needed some time to let it sink in. Once it did, the raw emotion of it all steam-rolled me. I knew something wasn't right, that there was more to this than merely a good story. There was a part of me hidden somewhere in there, something that resonated with my own experience. The process of self-discovery was painful, more so than I imagined.

I spend my whole life carrying other people's pain and sorrow, bringing hope and a vision of what could be. Yet my own soul wouldn't rest until I dug deep within myself and addressed my own pain, long buried and half-forgotten. I had to mourn and grieve for that which this experience has brought to the surface within me, to let go of past hurts and disappointments. I had to find hope and find it somewhere in this monumental story. I had to share the story of Ennis and Jack with anyone who would listen, as though through the recitation, they will continue to live and to be present among us.

Gradually the sharpness of this emotion softened, and a growing sense of peace emerged as I came to terms with life after this experience. As I take stock and realize how it has changed me, made me more sensitive to the needs of others, made me more aware of the fragility of the humanity we all share, and made me more open to the power of love in my own life, then and only then, can I look back on these difficult, painful moments and give thanks that I have come through them. I bid you peace.

Michael, 35, is an Anglican priest. His partner Peter is an actor. They both live and work in Britain. Michael posts using the screen name of Titus.

Painfully Real

—"Ennis del Mar"

While Annie Proulx may have intended to write a story about the destructiveness of homophobia, I think she wrote something else of which perhaps even she was unaware—a story about the destructiveness of emotional and physical abuse and the neglect of young boys. Though external and internal homophobia may have been the political message, the significance for me was the lasting effects of two childhoods void of parental support or love. While Ennis is fairly forthright about the circumstances of his early life and tells us about losing his parents and never finishing high school, Jack only tells us that his father showed him little interest and how nothing he did could please his old man. It's only later, when we meet John Twist, that we realize what unbearable cruelty Jack must have suffered as a child. Both Jack and Ennis were born, if not under a curse, then under a cloud; and although they enjoyed fleeting moments of passion and joy, without an underpinning of love, they had no idea where to take it from there. Had both

Jack and Ennis had childhoods built on love, I'd like to believe they would have had the means to make things work, or at least make better choices. Without that foundation, they were doomed from birth.

What *Brokeback* has done for me is to make me face all the hurts I have caused others (and they are legion) and the regrets of my life (too numerous and some too painful to remember). While I have taken small steps to rebuild relationships in my family, and although my family has been receptive, I'm still haunted by things I have said and done. While I can say, "I'm sorry," I can't undo how I feel. I have a regret for almost every day of my life, and most cannot be undone.

I still find myself crying at inopportune times. The only way I can prevent this is to not think about the story. When I'm awake, I can block it out of my mind for a time and get on with my life. Yet months after seeing this film, I still wake up most mornings hearing the music of the film or seeing Jack or Ennis. This hit me particularly hard one day when, in the first waking moment, I saw the face of Jack, broken, defeated, and resigned as he watched Ennis drive out of his life for the last time. No "Good-bye." No "See you in November." No "I love you." I spent the day paralyzed by heartache and tears.

As a child, I may have fantasized about movie characters and situations, but I never lost sight of the fact that movies weren't real. What surprises me is how real these characters are. Even though I know these characters are fictional, I still find myself wanting to track down the Twist family ranch and to dig up Jack's ashes and deliver them to Ennis or spread them on *Brokeback Mountain* myself.

To hell with John Twist.

Real life has almost never felt this painfully real.

A World That You Believe In

—Charlotte Graham-Clark

How can I, how can we, care so damn much for two people who aren't real? When I read a book or see a story that makes an impression on me, it becomes a permanent part of my memory, and I return to it repeatedly pretty much from that point on. It was in thinking of this, juxtaposed with the memory of my long-dead father, that I began to formulate a rather strange idea: after a certain point, the distinction between reality and fantasy begins to fade. It all becomes a function of memories and certain token objects that stir them. Just because I will never meet a favorite character from a story doesn't mean he or she isn't real. My father was real, but what's left of him? Memories and [the] objects that stir them. How is that different from a story that puts you into a world that you believe in, and love, for as long as the story lasts? "A difference that makes no difference is no difference."

Ennis and Jack were real, though we will never meet them. Ennis and Jack are gone. All that's left of them are the words and the pictures, but that doesn't mean that I, or you, will ever love them any the less.

Because they did exist; and they always will—in our minds and hearts.

Charlotte Graham-Clark, 46, is a potter, poet, and writer from Virginia who loves to travel. She posts under the screen name royandronnie.

Siddhartha's Smile

—Bianca Pulungan

There's a little story that I would like to share. It's from a book by Herman Hesse, *Siddhartha*. Near the end of the story, Siddhartha's friend looks upon him and sees his face. In that one second he sees the face of a baby, an old man, a fish, a murderer, a nobleman, a naked woman, and the faces of the gods Krishna and Agni—all forms and faces in a thousand relationships to one another. All these forms and faces rested and flowed, and the next thing he saw was Siddhartha's smile. Right then he knew how the Perfect Ones smiled. I really liked this scene from the book, and I always wondered about that smile, that smile with "no definition"—how does it look?

This movie touched my higher consciousness. In fact, this movie is the higher consciousness, and it took me into it. It's as if all my knowledge disappears, and I'm just like a little child. I see everything just as it is—without prejudice, without assumptions, and without judgment. In this state of mind, I see the purest love between two human beings. It is a picture of love with no example, no experience, and no clarity. It comes from a very vulnerable place.

I feel really blessed, and I want to thank Ang Lee for convincing me that art is doing good for humankind. Also, a thank you for everybody who was involved in *Brokeback Mountain* for showing me what Siddhartha's smile looks like.

Bianca Pulungan is a dancer from Jakarta, Indonesia, and has taught dance to children there. Recently, she, her husband, and little son moved to Germany so that she can continue her dance studies there.

I Am Different

—Robert Baxter

Last month, I came out to my mother. She's ninety-three! Of course she knew—of course. I come from the Jack and Ennis era. We didn't talk about it for lots of reasons, but my dear mother asked me why I was so upset. I told her that some of my friends had committed suicide forty years ago because their parents rejected them after learning they were gay. Yes, they did.

"I am different," my mother replied. God bless her, and God bless *Brokeback Mountain* and everyone who brought it to the screen. The miracle continues.

Robert Baxter, 66, is an award-winning journalist, arts critic, and opera lover from Cherry Hill, New Jersey. He posts under the screen name of Tacitus.

6 The Elephant in the Room

—Betty Greene Salwak

This movie has forced me to take action. I recently wrote the following letter to my church's pastor who is in charge of Christian Education. I am also a staff member at this church.

The Elephant in the Room

It's there. Everyone can see it, but no one will say anything. If we ignore it, maybe it will go away. Its presence makes some people uncomfortable. Maybe someone will make it go away. But it never leaves. The elephant is homosexuality.

To most heterosexual people, it remains easy to ignore as long as no one points it out.

But homophobia is not benign. It can do harm, even maim, both psychologically and physically.

It can take away your family, your friends, your job, and your self-respect; it can even kill. Homosexuals must be careful not to reveal themselves to American hate culture.

How did some in the Christian community attach themselves to this malevolence? How is it they ignore Christ's teachings to love one another? If we accept the grace given freely by God, how can we do less than offer grace to all of those around us—whether it makes us uncomfortable or not?

My brother was a victim of homophobia. He died ten years ago from AIDS. For most of his life he never came out to his own family. He was so afraid of being rejected outright that he chose instead to remove himself from us. We deduced he was gay from when he was in his early twenties—shortly after he annulled his brief marriage.

But for years no one said anything. It was the elephant in the room whenever we saw him for his brief and infrequent visits. He was tense and quiet during our times together. I learned later from his friends that he was especially fearful of my reaction because I am a Christian. The faith that has drawn me closer to all people created a distance between me and my brother.

It was not until he was hospitalized with Hodgkin's Lymphoma that our family learned he was HIV-positive. Shortly thereafter, he was placed in hospice care. He suffered increasingly from dementia, but he had some lucid moments. I was able to visit every three weeks during his last six months, for three days at a time. Sometimes he didn't know I was there, but other times we were able to talk. It was during one of those lucid times that I was able to tell him that our family had known he was gay for many years. We loved him and we didn't care whom he loved.

He changed before my eyes from a tense and unhappy man to one who was open, loving, smiling. He was free to be himself. I had never known this man before, and I knew him only for a brief time. It was a gift that I cherish. But homophobia robbed our family of the relationship we could have had.

We need to talk about homophobia. By talking about it, we can diminish its ability to do harm. An aspect that has always drawn me to our church is its willingness to discuss difficult topics in an open and thoughtful way. We have the responsibility to begin the conversation, because by being quiet we yield power to homophobia.

One way to begin this conversation is to talk about the movie Brokeback Mountain. *It provides a forum through which we can explore our reactions and discuss our responsibilities as Christians to the disenfranchised homosexual community. The movie clearly shows the disastrous results wrought by homophobia. Can we at least talk about it?*

My pastor and I spoke today about this letter. He agrees that the subject is one that we need to talk about. Our denomination (Presbyterian) is making some changes at the national level to support the ordination of homosexuals. This is big, folks, if somewhat belated. It's making official what's been going on unofficially (and unsanctioned) for years.

Our own church is in the middle of expanding, and one of the new spaces will house a large video room. There are plans to begin a regular "movie night" in the new space, and our pastor said that we might show *Brokeback Mountain*. I told him that the movie has the power to do something important, and since he hasn't seen the movie, I would be glad to lend him my copy.

No promises, but he acted interested and accepting. We are definitely going to have the discussion forum whether or not we show the movie. Our concern, of course, is the same one faced by the moderators of this Forum: we want to have a thoughtful discourse where we can respect each other's point of view.

Don't let the hatefulness of some believers get you down. God is at work here, changing the hearts of many through this wonderful movie. I truly believe that. And today, on the ten-year anniversary of my brother's death, I am proud to honor his memory with this post. Here's to you, David. I love you.

Betty Greene Salwak is a 52-year-old Sunday School director who lives in Indianapolis with her husband and two teenage children. She posts under the screen name of neatfreak.

7 Some Sweet Life

—Carol O'Brien

My husband is a great guy, but we never had that spark. Not even when we were dating. He was my best friend, though—we got along great, just not in the bedroom. But I was willing to let all that go for the safety of being with someone I loved.

In 1998, I went to a website for my favorite band. That's when I met Heidi. We talked a bit online, then on the phone, and then she invited me to come to Indiana to see a concert. I was excited, but scared. I'd never flown east of Las Vegas, and never by myself. I was scared to fly, but I was going to meet her and other girls, so I decided to go. We struck up a great friendship. We had so much in common. It was wonderful. She was funny and pretty and a great mom, and I admired all that. But then things started to change. We grew closer. Her husband flew me out as a surprise for her birthday. I got there, and she was in tears. Then I realized I was crying too.

We went to a basketball game that night, and as her hubby drove us home, she sat in the backseat with me and held my hand the whole way. We couldn't be physically parted. That night, when I went to get ready for bed on the couch, we sat down to talk and held hands and then couldn't stop. We kissed, and it was magnificent. This was what I had been missing all my life.

That was in 2000. For the next five years we agonized as our Almas either put up with us or didn't. We never meant to hurt anyone, but we couldn't help what we were doing. We were in love. She and her husband divorced. I tried to hang on with mine. Guilt was severe. My husband is a good man, and I wanted to make sure that I had done everything I could.

Then *Brokeback Mountain* burst into our lives.

Heidi saw it first. She called me crying and upset a lot over the next few weeks. I didn't get to see it until after Christmas, but the holidays were very stressful for us. She wanted me, come hell or high water. She was Jack, wanting our little cow and calf operation. I was Ennis, fearful—not of being gay (I've always been around gay people and had many gay friends), but of leaving my marriage, my job, my home, my family, to move to be with her.

Then I saw the movie.

I went by myself, afraid of my reaction. I had seen the trailer and cried my eyes out, so I knew it would be powerful. Let's say I had no idea. I felt like a ton of bricks had fallen on me. This was my life! I was shaken. I cried for days. I thought of nothing else. The worst part was, I missed so much of the movie by crying, so I knew I had to see it again. And again. And again. Four times in the theater; those were four of the most moving times of my life.

I tried therapy. My husband and I talked. I finally realized I could not go on living this double life. We agreed to divorce, and, luckily, he is such a good man that he and I are friends, still living in the same house, not arguing over who gets what, and we still sit and watch *The Sopranos* and movies together, and he wishes me well, as I do him. After eleven years, our marriage is over, but our friendship isn't. It never will be.

I called Heidi—my Jack—and said yes to that little cow and calf operation.

So now, packing and moving commences. I am forty-four years old and have lived in the same area my whole life. My whole family is here. My parents just moved into a retirement home, and I worry about them, but I can be home in half a day if I have to.

In twenty-nine years of employment, I have never left a job without having something else lined up. I have lived in this safety cocoon my whole life, and now I'm a butterfly, ready to leave the cocoon and change everything I know and have done because I love this woman and her children so much. It's been tough telling people, especially my family, but I have been supported graciously and given so much love and encouragement that it's been amazing.

Because of this movie. Because of Jack and Ennis. Because Annie wrote the story, and Larry and Diana wrote the screenplay, and Ang directed it, and Jake and Heath and Anne and Michelle starred in it. Because of all of this, I'm going to leave that lonesome trailer and go live on a "ranch" with my Jack.

It is going to be a sweet life.

Carol O'Brien is a 44-year-old medical records clerk from Indiana, who shares her life with her partner, Heidi, and their four children. She posts under the screen name Imennisshesjack.

Ennis thought he'd never had such a good time...

8 The Long View

Heavy Cross
—Matteo Z. Ferolie

I was raised a Christian but am not affiliated with any organized church.

However, one afternoon I was looking at a still picture from *Brokeback Mountain* when something about my early Christian orientation seeped out of my unconscious, and I was seized by a surprising awareness that Heath as Ennis and Jake as Jack performed a very Christly favor for me.

They had taken up my cross for me; they wore my crown of thorns by acting out my passion, my love, my sweet body-to-body, spit-swapping, deeply physical homoerotic love. Their awarenesses were my awarenesses, their sorrow and pain my sorrow and pain. They walked upon my Via Dolorosa, my way of sorrow.

These two strong, cowboy-butch, masculine guys, who loved each other passionately, somehow did that for me—and for how many other countless gay guys?

They lifted the heavy cross I've borne so many of my gay years and took it upon their shoulders, up there on the giant silver screen, and I knew, experienced, a sense of tremendous relief!

Matteo Z. Ferolie, 65, is retired and lives and works part-time as a salesman on Staten Island. He posts under the screen name Zadoc.

This Moment in Time

—Garry_LH

What is it with this movie? It keeps kicking me around. It's like everything I shoved away, just so I could survive, has decided to visit me in full measure. All I got are fragments, dreams of what might have been in my own life—if only I hadn't spent the first half of it as Ennis without a Jack.

Coming out politically first, before developing the support of other gay friends, is not something I'd recommend to anyone. But I've always been one who plunged headfirst once I made up my mind. I've got to bless those crazy religious zealots who tried that "no special rights" campaign here in Missouri several years back. If not for them, I would probably still be going from one half-assed Jack-and-Ennis relationship to another.

During that time, being openly gay while working at the local farm co-op with a Southern Baptist minister was interesting. I finally had to get to the point of telling him, "If your God doesn't like me, I guess I'll have to find one that does." Add in a car wreck, a near-death experience, and a year to get to where I could button a shirt again, this mourning process I'm going through is one bitch of an unsatisfactory situation. However, I still have to say, I'm damn glad it finally is happening because the truth is, I was headed into a downward spiral that sure wasn't pretty.

Then why did it take me being able to mourn the lives of these two fictional characters to let me do this for myself? I'm still too close to this fire to grasp this myself. For the first time in my life, I have a film that speaks in a dialect I can understand. (I love these posts from both coasts asking, "What did they say?") Here, I have a movie in which I don't have to transpose the love interest so that I can feel what it means for these characters. And not only do I know the characters in *Brokeback Mountain* by different names, but also most of them could be my relatives.

I don't know why it took Annie Proulx six months to write these thirty pages. Perhaps it was the ghosts of men who wanted their story told as a way to help those who now follow their path? Why did this brilliant script languish for nine years? Why did those who tried to get this movie made before fail to pull this project together? The answer in my own heart is that the spirit of *Brokeback* waited until it could pull in the right director and the right actors (who have done such an unbelievably real job of bringing Jack and Ennis to life). Everything had to wait for this moment in time. I feel that in twenty years we will look back and say, "Here is where things finally began to change. Here is where those who claim bigotry as a religious right were shown for what they really are."

It is because this movie seems to speak deeply to only some of its audience that I feel this brilliant film may be more of the realm of Spirit than its more mundane counterparts. For some of us, it is as though this movie has been sent so that we can let go of our own shadows. For if this movie has one message, it is "Grab life by the horns and ride it for all it is worth" because life is [as] short as the flesh is mortal. Make every moment count, and in the end, you'll know life has been good.

Honest, Grateful Tears

—Pierre

The credits roll, and I hurry to grab my coat and straighten my baseball cap, fearful that every emotion I was laughing off to myself, in order not to let them out, would pour out in the lobby. I couldn't look anyone in the eye for fear I would not know how to speak to them. I stumble out, confused, with a piercing pain in my chest and stomach. My phone rings, and I find it hard to breathe and speak to my ex on the line. I huff out, "I just saw *Brokeback Mountain*, and I really can't talk right now," and, after pauses while thoughts and scenes are crossing my mind, I hang up.

I tried to rationalize what I had seen, declaring that it's only a film; and I'm silly to let it physically affect me like this, but that was fruitless. All the pain, fear, and love I had always denied myself were just exposed to my eyes in a way I could not avoid or try to overlook any longer. I cried the hardest I had in years—truthful, necessary, honest, grateful tears. After my tears started flooding rivers, I promised myself to show thanks somehow for the miracle I had witnessed. I will never forget this. A film so beautiful, I could never find enough words to fully encompass my gratitude for showing me the beauty of life. I believe a flower is more beautiful when it grows in the sand than when it grows in the grass. The one place everyone expects beauty not to be is the one place it may need to be the most. I thank this entire miracle of a production for showing me a beauty in life and in myself where I thought it couldn't be, for showing life with its triumphs and its mistakes, and for making me believe that I'm not a mistake and that I'm deserving of more than a life of unhappiness for being who I am.

God bless *Brokeback Mountain*.

Pierre, 26, is a manager who lives in Brooklyn, New York.

Wouldn't Change a Thing

—City Girl

Pre-*Brokeback*: shopping, dining out, getting stuff done at work, a social life

Post-*Brokeback*: messy house, dirty clothes, bad hair, friends who think I'm insane, regular emotional breakdowns

. . . and I wouldn't change a thing.

Grace, 46, works in financial services and investments and resides in San Francisco, California. She writes under the screen name City Girl.

Priceless

—Moonbeam

Cost of movie tickets: 42 dollars (for 6 showings)

Weight gained by a diet of popcorn, Junior Mints, and Cherry Coke: 7.3 lbs.

Boxes of Kleenex to dry unexplained bouts of crying: 4

Money spent on E-bay on "I (heart) gay cowboys" t-shirt: 13 dollars (plus 5 dollars shipping)

Believing in love again as I watch the "dozy embrace": Priceless

Observation and Intuition

—greylocke5

Let me repeat why this movie hits some people so hard, myself included. It is not made like standard Hollywood movies, even tragedies about thwarted or unfulfilled love. Most movies tell you what to think and feel; they do not let your heart and mind figure things out. However, in real life you figure things out about other people through observation and intuition.

Richard, 55, is a retired civil servant who lives in northern Virginia. He posts using the name greylocke5.

A Spiritual Experience

—brokebackLJ

B*rokeback Mountain* is a spiritual experience for a lot of us; it's like a key that unlocked a certain part of our soul/heart/inner feelings in a way that can't really be explained. The "*Brokeback* Effect," I think, is only meant for certain people. Those people treat it almost religiously, which is a beautiful thing. I feel as if I'm a new person, reborn on a certain emotional level. Most of us who love this movie seem to be at a crossroads, moving to a different place (whether new or old) in our lives, a place we've been trying to get to, get out of, or understand. This movie helps bring us closer to understanding ourselves, which I think is the point of great art.

"Severe Emotional Wounding"

—Joseph Denney

A lot of people (myself included) have been confused and a little freaked out by their strong emotional reactions to *Brokeback Mountain*; to wit, the tears that seem to come almost non-stop in the weeks after first seeing the movie or reading the book and that seem to kick right back in at the drop of a cowboy hat in the months that follow. Some have said it felt like *Brokeback Mountain* uncovered a bottomless well of sadness in them that they didn't know existed (which also applies to me). What didn't make sense to me was why people with seemingly little in common (male or female, straight or gay, happily married or divorced, single or partnered) all ended up the same way, sobbing as if our hearts would break.

Well, I was re-reading Annie Proulx's "Getting Movied" essay in the *Brokeback Mountain: Story to Screenplay* book last night, and I ran across one sentence that leapt off the page at me. In the essay, Annie talks about her first meeting with Ang Lee, when she was still worried about whether he would be able to do the story justice, and how after they had spoken, she began to believe "he might be able to show the grief and anger that builds when we must accept severe emotional wounding." Those words, I think, are the key to why most, if not all of us, have experienced the same overwhelming emotional response to *Brokeback Mountain*, no matter what our personal history.

I think each of us who has had this reaction has experienced severe emotional wounding that, up until now, has never been healed by grieving. I also think the reason we had not grieved up until now is that the wounding (even though severe) was a slow process, so slow that many of us didn't even know we had been hurt until we saw the indisputable proof laid out before us on the screen or the page and realized that, to varying degrees, it was the story of our wounding being told.

Joseph Denney, 50, is a paralegal living in Los Angeles, California. He posts using the screen name WLAGuy.

"Exhaust Every Possibility"

—Sharyn Casapulla

Here's a quote from Jake I really liked. When asked what was the best advice he was given, he said, "Chris Cooper told me, 'Never have any regrets.' After Chris said that to me, I now walk into every scene thinking, 'Exhaust every possibility.'

Once you get to a certain place, it's like you just deliver everything you've got. Don't have any regrets." While he was talking about acting, he was also talking about life. I challenge us all to live each day exhausting every possibility! We owe it to Ennis and Jack, but especially to ourselves.

Sharyn Casapulla, 30, is an account executive, living in Falls Church, Virginia. She posts under the screen name Sharyn.

Self-Love

—gblady

First a bit of history, as I think it's pertinent to what I have to say. I am a fifty-seven-year-old, divorced, straight woman with two teenaged sons who just happen to look and act totally like Ennis and Jack. One is strawberry blond, stocky, extremely closed and private, while the other is dark-haired, lanky, and a totally extrovorted dreamer.

I worked seventeen years in a hospital urgent care setting on Capitol Hill in Seattle, which is the gay district, and many a shift, I was the token straight person (or TSP as I was affectionately called). I lived with a lesbian couple for a while, and I have tried and tried to understand the experience of being homosexual. I don't. As a wonderful co-worker, a lesbian mom with ten kids told me, "And you won't because you're not." I have great compassion and believe in personal freedom on all levels and the right to express that, but I don't get it to the point that I can understand the attraction. I guess I say this to show that I have had a deep level of connection with many people who are homosexual—saving lives shoulder to shoulder is pretty intense—and yet, I don't get it.
The first time I saw it [*Brokeback Mountain*], I didn't cry; I thought it was beautiful, tender, savage, and deeply moving. I did think it was slow. A great movie, end of story—so I thought.

This time when I saw it, I was devastated. I felt like I'd been slugged in the stomach at the realization that I was Ennis. For me, it was all about the isolation, the abandonment, the being terrified, and the hating myself and who I am. I was hounded, obsessed, and totally consumed; and I was so thankful that I found Dave's Forum. I did lots of soul-searching, crying, writing, and trying desperately to figure out why I was so crazy for *Brokeback*. Why couldn't I get my fill? What in me needs expression?

Two of my dear friends were very surprised that I identified so closely with Ennis. "But you don't act anything like that," they said. I thought to myself, "I'm a damned good actress." My outer demeanor is very different, but inside—wow! I came to realize I had kept it under wraps, even from myself, until watching myself in Ennis being laid out on the big screen. Over the next several days, I made the hugest inner change of my life. I was able to move from the frightened, scared Ennis to the Ennis who knew love. This is huge for me; I can't even find words to express how huge.

To me, it is not a gay movie. For me, that is not the main issue. For me, this movie was about love, and, personally, about self-love. My life at this point has been seemingly totally transformed by this movie, and I cannot begin to adequately express how grateful I am. I love myself! I have "a love that will never grow old" for myself; no one is ever going to love me like me—for the first time in fifty-four years. (I was three when I was abandoned by my mother, which is when the self-loathing started.) To me, it's an absolute miracle. It's a healing that years of therapy weren't able to do. Did I say how totally grateful I am?

So, I will keep my interpretation of what *Brokeback* is about for me because it is so incredibly sacred to me. There are no reins on this one, and I feel so blessed that it is so.

Waiting All My Life

—amdaz

Tell you what, as someone said earlier, I have been waiting to see this movie all my life. I was ready. All of my life experiences—the joy and the sorrow, people I met and lost, places and wonders I've seen—made me ripe for *Brokeback Mountain* in all of its glory.

Dean, 42, lives in Palm Springs, California, and posts under the screen name amdaz.

Tattooed on our Souls

—Paul Wheelock

This movie is part of my skin. What can I do? The emotional residue of the movie is as important as the movie. We will carry this movie throughout our lives because it is unlikely that something this significant will occur on film again during our lifetimes. We can look back during our lives at the time when *Brokeback* came out, the indescribable ways it affected us, and the quicksilver reasons we were changed. So take a deep breath and look around you. This is one of those few times in life that are life's mileposts. Although tattooing *Brokeback Mountain* on your skin is a wonderful expression of the lifetime effect of the movie, we all will be carrying it with us forever tattooed on our souls.

Paul Wheelock, 54, is a college Professor from Syracuse, New York. He posts under the name of 1224butternut.

9 Finding Control

—Dana Lankford

I grew up in Jackson, Wyoming, before there was a ski area. It was a way of life to hunt for your dinner. I was never very happy about it, but you had to step up and provide food for the family. The first elk I shot I had to dress with a pocket knife. My stepdad didn't trust me with a hunting knife. When I walked back to camp to tell them I had shot an elk, they didn't believe me because I didn't have blood up to my elbows. But I did a right proper job of it, and I kept clean. They should have known I was gay then!

My mom used to have dozens of wild game cookbooks. I have never liked antelope unless it was grass fed. Sagebrush fed is pretty nasty. Bear is greasy. My favorite is moose. Now they have made it so hard and expensive to hunt that I use that as an excuse not to.

My mom was a damn good shot, unless she tried to load her lipstick in the rifle. Mom was shooting at an elk and got the pockets mixed up that she kept her lipstick and her shells in. For a lady who never cussed, she got pretty rank for a minute until she figured out the problem. Later, when she would get out of line, we would remind her of the "lipstick incident."

Another Mom hunting story: after my dad passed, my mom started dating a game warden. Somehow she managed to get a rare license to hunt moose in a special area. She went out with my oldest brother to hunt. She found a two-year-old bull and shot it while my brother slept. He woke up and cleaned the moose. Four guys stopped by and threw it into the truck for her. We were impressed with her moose, but she just complained that she had broken a nail.

When I was growing up, beef was a luxury. I grew up on elk, but it has been years since I have eaten any. Now they eat my trees. I planted 103 conservation trees for a windbreak, and the elk had a buffet diner. All I had left was a yard that looked like that movie *Holes*. Around town, elk are like pets, until the bucks go into the mating season. Then you'd better look out. I see the tracks in my yard almost every morning. Today a buck stopped me on the street and he wouldn't move. He just gave me a look like I was driving on his street and he didn't appreciate it!

The last century has changed the country around here in Wyoming a fair amount, but maybe not as much as most of the world. I think it has to do with the harshness of the landscape. A lot of people who come here don't appreciate the wild sheer majesty of this part of the world. That is what I love about it the most. I have to say that when I am around large groups of people I am apprehensive, but when I am in the middle of a ground blizzard I feel comforted. I don't know what to expect from people, but, while this country is unforgiving, if you respect it, then you will be rewarded with wonders beyond belief.

I'm in my forties now. My lover and I built a cabin in the mountains and had a fevered love affair for many years. He was married and the only time we could have together was at the cabin. He left his wife and we moved in together, until he decided that he couldn't handle the thought that we might be found out. I moved out and started my life over from there.

For a long time I couldn't bring myself to even try and love someone else. When I first saw *Brokeback Mountain*, I realized that I had to open myself to others. I think the reason I have been so affected by the movie is that it has opened my eyes to my situation and given me the courage to step back into life.

One problem for my ex and me was that he didn't come out until he was forty-eight. I had sown my wild oats when I was young, but he wanted to catch up! One night he told me that I better get checked, because he had the clap. I didn't have it, so he didn't get it from me, and he was putting me at risk. When I realized that my boyfriend was having unprotected sex with other men, I shut down. I was too nervous about what he might come home with.

I am having a different take on *Brokeback Mountain* now. Yes, I do mourn for lost opportunities, but I have also found a new sense of control. I have been in a dysfunctional relationship for the past eight years. I am a Jack with a lover who is a diehard Ennis. I have changed everything in my life to accommodate him, and it has never been enough. But when I offer him his freedom, he becomes the most attentive man a man could want. Like Ennis, he will say how we can't be together, but he still sends me postcards when I'm not there.

I can't even get him to watch *Brokeback Mountain*, because he doesn't like sad movies. If anyone needs the positive message of this movie it would be him. I can control my life, but others have to find their own paths.

The control I have found is that I have broken it off with him. I am living my life for today and not for what could happen. I have even planned a vacation in the mountains without him. We always spent our vacations somewhere he wanted to go, but this summer I am going to enjoy my own obsession and explore the Big Horn Mountains.

A few days ago I visited Porcupine Falls, which is near Brokenback Mountain in the Big Horns. (This Brokenback has an "n" in it.) On the way back up, I lost my footing and fell. I knocked over a rock and there was one of those lapel buttons underneath. It was all rusted up, but I could read the inscription: *Are We Over the Rainbow Yet?*

Dana Lankford, 46, a life-long Wyoming resident, works for the railroad and loves all forms of outdoor life, including building cabins in the mountains. He posts under the screen name Wyomen.

10 Surviving Fraternity Row

—kaboyz

January 20, 2006:

I am twenty-seven and have lived in Long Island, New York, all my life, except for my college years. My father left my brother, mother, and me when I was just seven. He left us to be with his male lover of five years. My mother unconsciously raised us to hate him and gays. I realized I was gay when I was pretty young. But I did everything in my power to be nothing like my "faggot father."

I still don't have much respect for him. He didn't make a solid attempt to be a part of our lives while we grew up. When I first came out, my father's reaction was hope that this new bond would now somehow connect us—as if being my father wasn't enough.

I had girlfriends in middle and high school, but I also had secret deep crushes on male friends. I followed a girlfriend to college in West Virginia, but we broke up after a year there.

I joined a straight, Southern, military jock fraternity. During pledging, we had a pledge book, where we had to get interviews from every brother in the fraternity. Each one grilled us about 1) our family history, 2) their likes and dislikes, and 3) tasks they wanted us to complete, like cleaning their cars, cleaning their bedrooms, or standing in the cafeteria next to the milk dispensers and mooing loudly every time someone got milk.

Nearly every brother told me in these interviews that one of his top five dislikes was homosexuals. They would say "queers," "fags," etc. I felt like a fly on the wall. It was terrible. I got to see hate, ignorance, and racism firsthand. But I was invited, and I joined. For several months, I continued to try to be as straight as possible.

Then I met my Jack. He was in a rival fraternity and was absolutely adorable. We fell madly in love. When we first hooked up, I was living in the fraternity house and had two homophobic roommates. It didn't go over well at all.

Our first night together, when they discovered what was going on in my loft, they reported us to the fraternity president. He called my ex-girlfriend and told her I was extremely sick and she needed to get over to the house. She climbed up the ladder and peeked into my bed. She thought I was with a girl. I told her I was fine and asked her to leave and lock the door behind her.

The next day, two of my best friends, both straight, took me to a beautiful state park retreat that we went to almost every Sunday. We contemplated what in the hell I was going to do and worried about my safety. I dreaded the days ahead. At the time, I didn't know if my new boyfriend was ready to voluntarily make the same sacrifices I was being forced to make.

Fortunately he was.

That Friday, my fraternity met to determine my fate. They didn't want to scar their hetero-jock reputation, and they wanted answers from me. It was the most difficult situation I have ever been in. But for the first time ever, I was completely honest with a group of friends and with myself. For the previous three years, I had formed a strong brotherly bond, and that overrode the fact that I was gay. Out of about thirty-five of my brothers, only about five refused to be associated with me again.

Eventually, they realized and accepted that I was really no different than before I came out. Obviously, there were some struggles. They wouldn't shower with me in the communal shower; they were afraid I wanted them. My roommate moved out, and no one wanted to live with me. A few religious brothers spewed their beliefs at me.

But I was determined to advocate for myself. I made it my mission to fight the ignorance. They actually showed interest and curiosity about understanding what being a homosexual male was all about, and they were cool with me. Luckily for me, pretty much the entire football team was in my fraternity, and they were always looking for fights. So if anyone gave me trouble, my back was covered.

My boyfriend's fraternity wasn't as accepting as mine. They weren't aggressive about it, but they disassociated themselves from him. He left the college shortly afterwards. We were only together for about three months, but they were the most intense three months of my life. We were madly in love and didn't care who knew. This gave us both the courage to come out. When he got home, he came out to his family and friends, and this was terribly difficult for him.

Unfortunately, we both moved on to different places in our lives. I like to believe we were both absolutely heartbroken, but we never really spoke of it again. I moved on and met my second boyfriend, whom I have been with for the last five years now. I am fortunate for that! My mother didn't take to me being gay all that well. It took her at least three years to come to terms with it.

After going through a lot of therapy and finally accepting who I am, I am happy with being gay. It feels amazing not to be ashamed. I am glad society has become somewhat desensitized to it. I want equal rights and I hope they come soon.

I still think back to this friend from a few years ago. I can only imagine what I would do if I got a note from him saying he was in town and wanted to meet up. I have his email address, but have had little contact with him since our short tragic relationship. I feel compelled to email him to tell him that seeing *Brokeback Mountain* reminded me of our love affair back in West Virginia and I hope he is doing well. I think I might!

May 31, 2006:

So remember how I messaged my first love back in January? Well, I heard back from him! I just asked how he was and what he was up to. I am glad he responded.

The author is a 27-year-old man from Hauppauge, New York.

They were each glad to have a companion...

11 Our Brokeback Stories, Part I

For many people in the gay community, Brokeback Mountain *was the first mainstream Hollywood movie to reflect their realities. However, gay men were not the only ones affected by* Brokeback Mountain. *Many straight viewers were able to see their own stories reflected in this movie. In this chapter, viewers who were profoundly moved by* Brokeback Mountain *share their own stories.*

Our Story

—Jari Koskisuu

As a gay man, I realize that we lost the stories of previous generations to AIDS. It took away thousands and thousands of men who could have taught us and told us their stories. We weren't left without stories altogether because we heard incredible stories of pain, loss, love, sorrow, bravery, and commitment in the face of death; but we didn't get to share the stories of love and life. We had no frame of reference. We had to create stories without the wisdom of earlier generations and without affirming stories in the culture around us.

Now I know that there are millions of stories worth telling and sharing. Our stories have never been told. [We have] stories of love, lust, happiness, joy, betrayal, loss, tragedy, and pain—the stories to which we could relate and that would speak of us. *Brokeback* does that. It is a movie of basic humanity and choices, love and denial, but it is also our story.

Forty-four-year-old Jari Koskisuu, who lives with his partner in Helsinki, Finland, works in the rehabilitation field. He posts using the screen name Boris.

Putting Everything in Perspective

—John Trudell

I live in Bay City, Michigan. I'm forty-nine. I came out in 1974 when I was seventeen. I spent a lot of time in Wenona Park because there was nowhere else to go to meet people. I met my lover Alan there. We were together for a year and then on and off for fourteen years.

I was shyer back then than I am now. I hardly ever talked. Even with Alan, it took a few weeks. I remember the first night we had a really long conversation. He said it was the most he'd ever heard me talk.

Alan was an alcoholic. We had a few fights when he was drunk. More than once I got a bloody nose and a few bruises. I lost two teeth.

In a lot of ways I am like Ennis (quiet, afraid, and lonely), but in my life, it was Alan who had the uncontrollable rage.

He was married to Bonnie. Her father owned a furniture store, and she stood to inherit a lot of money. Alan told me that was why they got married. He never went to college, and he thought that would be the best way to have a decent life. It was all about the money.

He gave up on that idea quickly. They separated, and Alan went back to the Navy because it was the best paying job he could find. They ended up getting divorced, but even after that, he was afraid to let me come live with him. He was afraid of losing his Navy job if anybody found out. I drove down there when I heard about the divorce, and I drove back the same night, crying.

We saw each other a few times a year until 1988. He would usually come to Bay City, and we'd go Up North. He loved to fish. I would hitchhike or drive to Waukegan. I would not allow myself to get seriously involved with anybody for all those years, although I did have opportunities. I was waiting for Alan to ask me to come live with him.

The last time I saw Alan was the summer of 1988. We went up to the Rifle River. It was a nice weekend until Sunday afternoon when we were getting ready to leave. We had a big argument. I can't remember what started it, but I do remember asking him why he kept stringing me along, why he wouldn't just dump me so I could get on with my life. Alan tried to hug me when I was crying, and I pushed him away. I didn't talk to him for a long time after that.

I still have a jacket hanging in my closet that Alan gave me to wear one night. The last time I tried to call him, his phone had been disconnected. I heard from a friend a few months later that Alan had died. He said he had heard it from a friend, but wasn't sure since he had never seen an obituary. I didn't know where his parents had moved. Most of his friends that I knew were dead or had moved away.

In 1995 I typed his name on some Internet search, and an address and phone number popped up. It was a listing in Hersey, Michigan. I remembered that his parents had a summer place there. So I called, hoping. Alan's mother answered. She told me that Alan had died in 1989 from cancer.

I keep going back to the movie. Not because I enjoy remembering the pain, but because I feel so much better when I see Jack and Ennis together and happy. The last flashback, the "dozy embrace," always takes my breath away. Alan used to hold me and sing softly all the time.

Brokeback Mountain puts everything in perspective now.

John Trudell is a 49-year-old hotel controller and pianist from Bay City, Michigan. He posts under the name of BayCityJohn.

It's My Turn to Live

—mainebartender

Many years ago I lost someone special to me in a bike accident. I have come to realize that in all these twenty-plus years that I have been using him to judge all other men I have met, and none have measured up. I now know I have to let go of him and face life on my own. I still dream about him weekly. It's odd; he has aged all along in my dreams, and we are still best friends. At the time of his death, his family would not let me into the hospital room or attend the funeral.

Although he was seven years older, I was the one at fault for "messing up their little boy." I was angry for a long time, but now I have to let it go. I may be fifty-one, but I have a hell of a lot of living to do. Thanks, *Brokeback*. It's my turn to live.

These Words Would Haunt Me the Rest of My Life
—Mcnell1120

I had a close friend in high school; I met her in junior year. The only child of Polish immigrants, her parents were divorced. She had no friends. She was a tall, husky girl, not a gorgeous blonde, so I guess everyone thought she was too tough or ugly to hang around with. Well, that didn't stop me. In senior year, my other friends couldn't understand why I always included her in our activities because she just didn't fit in. We were all skinny, fashion-conscious, cute girls. We got all the guys. I always dragged her around. We shared our dreams together and our fears about our futures.

Eventually, my other friends began enjoying her. She was funny and made us all laugh. I loved her for who she was. She changed my outlook on life. I always wondered why she never talked about guys. Maybe she was gay? I don't know; I never cared and never asked. We graduated in 1984, and I remember the words she told me as we said our goodbyes and gave our hugs. "Hey, this Polaka loves you. You changed my life, and I'm so glad you accepted me for who I am. I'm so glad to have met you, crazy-ass Puerto Rican!"

I didn't know these words would haunt me for the rest of my life. We were getting ready for college. She and her mom were going to tour one of Wisconsin's colleges on a small plane when it crashed. Six of the seven people on board died. My friend and her mother were gone in the blink of an eye. Do you know what that did to me? I can't begin to explain.

Twenty years later, I sit here crying, but I feel good about myself because I was her friend. I took that chance of being taunted by everyone else. I wish I could continue to be courageous in today's world. Sometimes it's hard. For some reason, *Brokeback Mountain* brought that all back.

For twenty years I withheld my emotions about my only true friend, a friend who never had a chance to love. Through her eyes, I saw that movie with a different perspective. She died almost twenty-one years ago at the age of eighteen. Did she have a secret to tell me? I will never know. Her father continues to mourn for his only daughter, never having had the chance to walk her down the aisle.

As I sat there in the movie theater alone, her presence was there. I know that may sound freaky, but I often think about her and ask for her help, for advice that I feel she would have given me. God, how I miss her!

All Ennis had left were the two shirts hanging in the closet. All I can do is look at our high school pictures and read the backs of them. If only I had convinced her to stay in Chicago and go to college here. She wouldn't have gone on that plane. She would still be alive. No, I don't blame myself . . . anymore. It took twenty years to get rid of the guilt.

If I had gone to therapy for this, I would have spent thousands of dollars, but I would still feel empty inside. I've always been kind to people, but I have taken them for granted. I didn't know you could lose a friend so easily. I only knew her for two years, but it was a good two years. Damn!

Nellie, a 40-year-old married mother of two from Chicago, is an insurance adjuster who loves painting and photography. She posts under the name Mcnell1220.

There Was Nothing to Do but Try to Stand It

—Curt

I grew up in a small town in southeast Oklahoma. I always knew I would have to leave, and it tore me apart to have to decide between my home and family or a real life. Not all of my friends were as lucky as I was to make it out. I was only twenty-four when, in the wee hours of July 4, 1987, a close friend of mine from college was brutally murdered on a lonely country road just north of the Oklahoma-Texas border. Greg was a year younger than me. His murderer was never found.

The bumbling state investigators and local authorities retrieved a pair of blood-splattered blue jeans at the scene left there by the perpetrator. They must have had some idea of Greg's orientation because they tested his blood for HIV. It tested positive, sending ripples through every small town in the area. None of the crime scene investigators would work on the jeans. Their solution was to put the only DNA evidence they had into an autoclave and sterilize it. This, of course, ruined the jeans as evidence. This was only one of many injustices in this case.

Greg had just graduated and was teaching in a local high school. He was well known and liked. I was beginning to come out at the time within the relative safety of Dallas. My mother called to ask if I knew him. My parents' advice was to stay away from the funeral and not to make any inquiries. There were two other friends of Greg's in our clique. To all our shame, we stayed away. In those days, you lived your life in the nooks and crannies.

Greg had one close friend from his hometown. The investigators pegged him as the suspect based on a "lovers' quarrel" motive. Tim and Greg were childhood friends and were never romantically involved. When the authorities finished with Tim (also twenty-three), he was as dead inside as Greg. I never forgave myself not being there for him, but there was nothing to do but try to stand it.

I had buried these memories for all these years. Seeing Jack being chased down in Ennis's imagination jolted me. I was traumatized, and it took me weeks to work through it.

Wondering about Every Missed Turn of the Road

—Rebel

As a boy, I was blessed that my father took me camping and fishing in the Flattops Wilderness Area of northern Colorado. In this time with him, I learned to appreciate the world in its natural beauty. *Brokeback* takes me back to these places. They conjure emotions of connectedness, yearning, and humility. [I remember] those long summer days and starlit nights, telling stories around the campfire as the air begins to chill. The experience is palpable. I can smell the smoke, taste the elk meat, feel the damp cold, and hear the crackling embers.

There's a brief scene at the end of the film where Jack and Ennis are riding horseback along the banks of a small lake together at the end of the day—probably saying nothing to each other, letting the silence of the moment together fill the empty air with peace and familiarity that would be meaningless if it were not for the sharing of it.

It breaks my heart to think about Ennis five or ten years down the road, lying awake in bed late at night, trying to remember the shape of Jack's face by the flickering light of the campfire or the sweet smell of his skin as he lay curled up next to him in their tent under the stars all those endless nights, wondering about every missed turn in the road.

My father remarried twice after my mother, and I had to struggle through stepmothers and family relationships that never felt close. I've come to realize that I've never allowed myself to truly open up to someone else. I guess I'm guarded and fearful that someone else can never truly love me. In turn, I never truly love them back. It's frustrating that I know this about myself, yet I can't find a way to fix it.

A few years ago my father suddenly passed away. He drove to the convenience store by his ranch in Reno . . . because his shoulder was really aching. [He] picked up some ice to ease the pain, got back into the truck and had a heart attack right there. No warning.

My sister, who lived across the street from me, called in hysterics. I couldn't process her words until I got there and saw her face. I've never felt a grief so deep. I couldn't open my mouth to speak. All I knew was that everything was now different.

My brother and I took his ashes up to the mountaintop lake where he had taught us to fish as boys. It was one of the most important things I've ever done in my life.

Rebel is a native Nevadan and a cowboy at heart.

12   The Sum of Us

—Doug Carr

I am consumed. I am cursed. There are so many memories, so much pain. I had successfully buried most of it until this movie brought it all rushing back. I had actually convinced myself I was happy, doing okay.

With my first love, I was young and I was Jack. My Ennis, Ruben, was so afraid, but so loving and kind. He was a real cowboy. I had made my mind up we would live together and grow old together. He broke up with me by bringing in a minister, who for hours told me that I was evil, that I was ruining both my life and Ruben's. I was heartbroken.

But Ruben would not stay away. He would come back to me, only to accuse me of being his evil temptation afterwards. After three more times, I finally had to walk away, never to see him again.

With my second love, John, I was Ennis. I feared love, feared being hurt again, feared being his. He was kind and loving to a fault, a true cowboy from the hat to the boots. He was from my hometown, no less. I slowly fell deeply in love. Over the months, we dated, and then he was suddenly gone. No one knew what had happened. Turns out he was in the hospital all that time, dying from pneumonia. I finally found him. His sister and folks were there; his sister-in-law, a religious nut, was trying to get him to "confess his sins" so he could go to heaven. I threw that bitch out of his room, kissed him on the forehead, and told him I loved him and so did God. He died that night.

With my third love, Michael, I was a severe Ennis. He was a joy to be around, a true Jack in all respects, but not a cowboy. Very outgoing, while I had become introverted to the extreme. He was my light, my way of interacting, my everything. We had three good years, and two terrible ones. He was a Type One diabetic; after two years of severe insulin reactions, his diabetes finally got him in early 1993.

He loved Christmas; we always decorated the house and had many friends over during the holidays. I denied him his last Christmas, because his doctors told me he was doing this to himself. Later, it turned out that was not true, and I regret that decision so very, very much. He had his last grand mal seizure on January 6, 1993, as I was working in the next room. I heard him and found him completely cramped up. I dialed 911; he fought to stay home, though he was not really conscious anymore. He kept screaming, "Doug, help me! Help me!" as they took him out to the ambulance. I could only sit on the steps and cry. He died thirteen days later, never again awaking from his coma. He is buried on private land where no fags are welcome. I cannot visit.

I am too afraid and, frankly, too tired, to love anymore. I know the pain of having clothes of your loved one to hold: I have a closet full of them. I cry every time I dig out his pictures, or hear his voice on a recording. Years are flying by, and I cannot stop suffering.

I am so lost, so very alone.

I just got back in from milking ninety-five head of cows; I milk evenings for my neighbor. It gives me some time to think about what I have been feeling.

Brokeback triggers these memories for me. It showed me that I was rationalizing my feelings to make them go away. Then the good memories started to come back, the happy times. If I knew only what I knew then, I would have to make the same decisions again. How could it be different? Only hindsight makes it so rough. I am starting to feel in balance again.

While we mourn our loss, Ennis and I could not have made any decisions differently, or it would have been different in the first place. At the moment, when all is weighed, there can only be one answer. Be it right or wrong, it has to be. We carry the weight of our past, maybe much of the weight of our parents' past as well. That weight is going to change the balance of our decisions. While from the outside we can see flaws, it is impossible to see them from the inside. Later, one may work through enough to see the flaws, but at that point it is of no use to regret the earlier decision. One can only mourn the loss.

Perhaps that is one thing this movie does. It throws your balance so far off that you have to re-evaluate all your assumptions, changing the balance again. I know my balance has felt completely out of whack since I saw this movie.

It would be nice to be part of a crowd of gays, straights, bisexuals, and others, where all were accepted as fellow human beings. Maybe a movement could start from here. We are in desperate need in this country of changing Us or Them into All of Us Together.

Doug Carr, 50, lives on a ranch in Nebraska where he milks 100 cows daily and runs an internet-based business. He posts under the screen name Doug2017.

13 Beyond Appalachia: A Journey Out of the Closet

—Wtg02

As a gay man born and raised in a small town in the hills of southern Appalachia, the film stirred up my own *Brokeback* experiences. I think at some level I was horrified at the thought of who I might have become had I stayed in that small town. I dated girls all through high school and women all through college. I was active socially in my high school and community. However, growing up, when I heard someone use the word, "queer," a word spoken with venom and disgust, I was sure that was in the "not-me" category, even though I knew I had warm, affectionate feelings for some of my good male friends. Those feelings were probably much more lustful than I wanted to admit to myself. But more importantly, there was no language to talk about those feelings in any direct way, and as a consequence, it was as though part of me didn't exist.

My first love was a guy in my neighborhood during my teen years. Subsequent *Brokeback* experiences I had before and after I left Appalachia were quite exciting, often carried on in places as beautiful and isolated as *Brokeback Mountain*. There was an intense level of mutual emotional attraction, yet a delicate balance between intellectual and emotional closeness, as well as varying degrees of physical intimacy. But those relationships could only go so far. All of those men have since married women. I'm sure you can guess the painful endings. I said goodbye to many a "Jack" or "Ennis" in my early years. Feeling distraught, I would get on a plane and get on with life somewhere else.

I was unprepared for the intense emotional reaction I had to *Brokeback Mountain*. Memories of my own *Brokeback* experiences came rushing back. Every Ennis or Jack from many years ago returned to my consciousness. What I've come to understand is that not only were those relationships not very fulfilling—even though they were exhilarating—but there was never any real closure. Consequently, everything at the end seemed to be in a muddle. I was trying desperately to wrap my mind around what was happening. Yet, like Ennis, it was difficult for nearly all of those men to talk about what was happening for them, and what was happening between us. Without explanation or closure, I felt empty inside, longing for a deeper connection. I also wondered whether I would ever be able to have a sustained, meaningful relationship with a man.

The first time I told anyone I thought I was a homosexual was the summer of 1965. The word gay wasn't even part of the lexicon of my world then. I was 19 and in college, and quite sure I wasn't queer. I also never imagined that the process of coming out would be a lifelong journey in this culture. Nor did I have any idea how painful that process would be. What the film so poignantly portrayed for me is that living in the closet not only takes an incredible amount of psychological energy to monitor and censor your every word or move, but it robs you of being fully human, as we witness in Ennis.

I came out to my parents when I was 25 during graduate school at Tulane University. It wasn't easy at first, but my parents were very supportive, as they were throughout my life. Their love and encouragement allowed me to become the person that I am.

Brokeback Mountain has helped me see that I had to leave that small town in Appalachia to make a social-psychological space to accommodate my feelings and desires for men. And what coming out has meant as a lifelong journey has been to make that space ever larger.

At the beginning of this journey, I naïvely thought that telling people I was gay and somehow managing my fears regarding the homophobia in our culture would be my biggest obstacles. Although it became easier over time to tell people—and that in itself felt liberating—I had no idea that the biggest obstacle would be my own internalized homophobia.

We all have a story to tell, just as I'm sharing part of mine here. Our stories are fundamental to how we cognitively make sense of the world, how we know and understand one another through joy and suffering. Our stories are an integral part of how we make connections with one another. Our stories embody our hopes and dreams for a future of possibilities.

But how do you realize your hopes, dreams, and desires in a culture that denies or marginalizes, and ultimately refuses to legitimize your experiences? How do you realize hopes and dreams when you've internalized society's homophobic script, along with its underlying presuppositions about you, not just as a gay person, but as a human being?

Juxtaposed to the agonizing personal struggles of my earlier years mirrored in *Brokeback Mountain*, I've also experienced a good bit of joy in life, probably because I've experienced love—with family, friends, and of course with my partner. Three years ago my partner and I moved into a house that we designed and had built—a labor of love we worked on for many years. Our house is a symbol of the extraordinary twenty-five-year relationship we've had together.

What happened for us has been better than either of us ever imagined. With a great deal of respect for one another, we've created a very loving, caring, nurturing relationship. At the same time, we've helped each other wrestle with our own internalized homophobic demons. Together we've stepped out of the closet, making our relationship increasingly visible to the larger world. After twenty-five years, we continue to have passion about life and living and, most important, about one another.

So *Brokeback Mountain* has helped me appreciate the trajectory of my life, beginning so long ago in southern Appalachia. Despite the *Brokeback* experiences from my early years, and despite how cruel the culture can be, I also appreciate how enormously lucky I've been to share so openly such a deep abiding love with my partner.

You know I ain't queer.

14 Our Brokeback Stories, Part II

A Passion to Find Joy

—MSPJeff

I met my Ennis when we were dormmates during our freshman year in college. We lived together for five years and stayed in touch for three years afterward.

Initially, I think we both viewed each other with a sort of mutual infatuation, two thinkers who'd found each other as brand-new grownups on the "Island of Misfit Toys" that was the small college we were attending. We went on walks together and found excuses to get off campus together and into the real world as often as we could. By the end of our first year, we were finishing each other's thoughts and had arranged to be roommates when the semesters changed.

The next year, we moved to a larger state university and found an apartment together. We were buying books and albums for one another, planning weekend trips, and cooking meals for each other. I remember setting up a Christmas tree as a surprise that first year in the apartment and hearing his emotional rush of breath when he walked in to find it lighting the dark living room. He found me hiding in the next room, and as he bear-hugged me with tears in his eyes, I realized that we were in love.

As I grew more willing to admit and explore this, he became more reticent and resistant. I knew Mark felt what I was feeling; I could see him reeling from it and leaning into it all at once. However, small-town family upbringing prevented him from admitting to me or even to himself what he was experiencing, except by the most oblique, almost accidental, means. Once, we took a road trip from the Midwest out to New York. In the wordless, contented hours driving back through Ohio, he took [out] a placemat and some crayons we'd gotten at a roadside restaurant. [He] cuffed me on the shoulder to show me he'd written our initials inside a huge red heart. We held hands during the next few silent minutes, but eventually he grew uncomfortable, withdrew his hand, and scribbled over the heart.

So it went for years. The more I pushed to admit and grow what we'd found with each other, the more frightened and evasive he became. You could see it in his eyes, this childlike fear and reaction to what he constantly found himself feeling. The more certain I became of what was happening, the more impatient I became with his reluctance. Slowly our orbits spun further from center.

It took me a while longer to assign the word "gay" to what I, at least, was feeling. I think that pushed him over the slope. He had only allowed himself to think of us as best, "best friends." He not only started to date women, but also became disappointed when I wasn't encouraging or enthusiastic at his success. I didn't realize it then, but he was in full denial and reversal mode; and I was too far down my own path to ever want to follow. We stayed friends for years, yet my resentment at what I saw as his betrayal of something so eminently powerful darkened and grew. Even at that young age, I think I knew that something so strong, joyful, and deep was rare, precious, and not easy to come by.

The crowning blow was when he asked me to be the best man at his wedding. He knew how we both felt and what it would mean for me. It was the ultimate performance of this ridiculous cover story we'd been portraying. It shredded my heart. What hurts more than his asking is my following through with the charade. I told myself it was an act of love at the time, but as the years pass, I see it more and more as a lack of confidence and self-assurance on my own part. It took me a long, long time to acknowledge to myself who I was, to come out to myself and everyone in my life, and to start to live from there.

I thought that coming out would remove the unseen obstacles and make finding love easier, but now at forty-two, I see that hasn't been the case. I've found plenty of this and that, but never anything approximating the heart-binder that started it all. I had begun to think that such completeness of love must only be for the young, but now this masterful movie and the story it portrays has awakened in me a passion to find joy and share it with someone as deeply and as long as possible.

MSPJeff is 43 years old and comes from Minneapolis, Minnesota.

Loving "Ennis"

—michelle

Over time, loving someone like Ennis, giving your all, over and over, to someone who just can't tell you what he's feeling because of the wall he's built around himself, wears you down until your heart burns itself out. This is especially true when the physical bond between you is so overwhelmingly strong. Even when survival dictates you throw in the towel and walk away, you always relent. With the tiniest glimmer of hope that his shell is cracking and the pain within is leaking out, you drop your defenses and rush to be there. So, you try again and again until the passion you felt burns down like the embers of a fire, and it becomes harder each time to revive it.

The reason this movie got to my core is because it let me see inside Ennis's head; it let me hear his pain cry out. My own Ennis is so stoic and closed up. Not only does he have no words for the pain, but he also won't even acknowledge it's there most of the time. It's the same with toothaches; he's terrified of the dentist and will let a tooth abscess until the tooth eventually dies. I usually don't know until his whole jaw starts to swell up.

I've fallen in and out of love with him so many times, had his children, left him twice (for their [the children's] sake—he's a drinker), and [have] always taken him back. He had a seriously fucked-up childhood, about which he never talks, but laid out the facts to me right after we met and when we first fell in love.

A few years ago, the children and I staged an intervention, which was incredibly painful for them because they love him so much. He spent a month in rehabilitation, during which he was forced to confront a lot of things about himself. It was also an outlet for my anger and a way for our children to tell us both how much pain they'd suffered. One more time we "torqued things" back to the openness of those first few blissful months. We went on the honeymoon we never had and recaptured something I thought had been dead a long time. Then it slowly all went to hell again because he closed up. "Nothing ended, nothing begun, nothing resolved." There's nothing worse than that.

Now the children are grown. All have become beautiful, loving human beings; three have families of their own. I am close to all of them. It kills me to see the love and disappointment in their eyes when they see their father so emotionally cut off, so set in his denial, and much frailer now. My Ennis also expresses himself in teasing, sometimes gently, but more often not. When attacked, he wields his wit into terrible sarcasm that can wound and cut you down. It's part of his defense system. If I left him, he'd end up like Ennis in that bus station. I did leave him once for three years, during which he lived in an apartment with no furniture, hardly ate, and mostly drank. Our eldest son, then seventeen and in his last year of high school, stayed behind, feeling he had to look after his father. They would have starved if he hadn't taken a job as a dishwasher in a hotel and been able to sneak some meals from the cook; how pathetic. Yet, his father is a teacher, beloved by his students, and a hard worker who never missed a day's work in his life, even when I was having our kids. He's a charmer to all who know him outside of our family, but living with him is like pulling teeth.

Michelle Tisseyre is a married 58-year-old novelist, translator, journalist and activist from Montréal, Québec in Canada.

Brokeback challenged some of us to face our own lives: to make changes, find old friends, think about what we really want from life.

Something Has to Change

—FinnInMinnesota

I am a sophisticated, reserved, silent, urban gay man with [a] razor-sharp tongue and forty-three years under my belt . . . .

Today I realized why *Brokeback Mountain* has had such an impact on me. It's about passion, love, and choices. I finally had to face mine. I always knew that I was gay, but I grew up in a rural area in eastern Finland in the 1970s, so I had nowhere to go and no one to ask what my feelings meant. I moved to a big city and finally met a guy in a bar when I was nineteen. He raped me. Bleeding, ashamed, bruised, and desperately alone (I couldn't face anyone or tell anyone), I decided that I would never ever again seek gay relationships or even the company of gays.

I ended up getting married to a workmate. Our marriage was a disaster, but when my wife miscarried, I realized that this couldn't be the life I was destined to live. I couldn't go on being married to a woman that I couldn't love and bring children into this world who would be hurt by my wounds. I was thirty, alone and scared, but I felt that I was adult enough, strong enough, and man enough to seek love and friendships with other men. It was difficult and painful in the beginning, but finally I met a guy who was patient enough, loving enough, and secure enough to show me what lovemaking can be. He was not capable of showing what love can be, but I will always be grateful for him. In his very physical way, he was capable of healing me with affection, tenderness, and patience.

I met my spouse a couple of years later, and we have been together for eleven years now. He is a beautiful, kind man. His beauty only increases as years pass by, and we are comfortable together. However, that is the problem; we are comfortable. There has never been passion or sharing like I had in my dreams. I chose a man and a relationship without risks. I chose security over love, affection over passion. I was afraid to feel love, to depend on someone, and to get hurt.

How do I know this? After being together for three years, I met another guy. Immediately, I felt something. We had a short but passionate, larger-than-life affair. It was incredible: [it was] a tender, physical and spiritual connection beyond anything I had been able to imagine. I left him. I felt that I had to. I could not do that to my spouse. My commitment and promises to him were more important. I remember our last evening together, walking on an empty street and feeling pain, unbearable pain. I howled. In my mind I did the right thing and have always thought so, until I saw *Brokeback Mountain*.

Now my spouse and I share our life together. It is not a bad life, but we have silently drifted apart. Last night I watched him sleeping and felt great tenderness and affection. However, at the same time, I felt shut in, incapable of reaching over the void between us and afraid to shake the status quo between us. I watched him breathe, and I realized that although I love him dearly, I have never loved him in the way he deserves to be loved, unconditionally as a whole. Once again I feel alone and scared.

Brokeback tore down all my defenses, my excuses, and the walls I had built around my soul. It made me naked and forced me to face my life as it is. I know that something has to change, but I don't know how to proceed. I have always been afraid of love, passion, real sharing, and being vulnerable. Now I realize what I have lost because of my fears.

An Epic, Tragic Love

—Titus

Ten years ago, I was working for my best friend and her husband. She was one of those beautiful Southern girls who have a magnetic charm. He was a brash, hard-nosed New Yorker (sorry New Yorkers!) [who was] all wound up, in control of everything, and so tight you could bounce a quarter off him. She had an affair and left him. He turned up on my doorstep in tears; I held him all night and, as if lightning had struck me, fell in love with a man I had never even looked at in such a light.

I moved in, helped raise his son, and nursed him through bouts of multiple sclerosis. We had a physical, affectionate relationship, but no sex because I knew that would end our relationship. I thought he would never have been able to cope with that. I sometimes shared his bed, held him, and soothed away his self-doubt and heartache in the aftermath of their divorce. He slept with every woman he could get his hands on, but he always came home to me. His girlfriends couldn't understand it; his wife resented me and will not speak to me to this day. Our families thought I had been the cause of the divorce. It was surreal.

After three years, I knew I needed more; I needed a man who could give me all of himself without reservation. I decided to leave the United States and come to the United Kingdom. He was against my going, but insisted on taking me to the airport. It was difficult saying goodbye like that. He hung around and around until I thought he'd never go. Then as the plane began boarding, he pulled me aside from the queue and took off his suit jacket and gave it to me, saying,

"Ought to look your best for your interview," and then pulled me close and held me so long I thought my heart would break. Then he kissed me, which he had never done before, and watched me disappear onto the plane. I cried all the way across the Atlantic.

My Ennis wasn't gay, not even bi-curious, as far as I could see, but he knew that my love for him was real, deep, and true. It amazed him, and he respected it. I loved him. It was an epic, tragic love that knocked me down and turned my life inside out, and sometimes it still hurts.

I have a wonderful life now and a man (whom I wouldn't trade for anything in all the world!) who loves me beyond all imagining, but this movie has brought back that bittersweet time when I loved someone who could never take that step, take my hand, and love me, too.

Michael, 35, is an Anglican priest. His partner Peter is an actor. They both live and work in Britain. Michael posts using the screen name of Titus.

15 He Could Cook, Too!

—Jim Titzman

First, I want to say that I'm pretty much an Ennis person. I grew up during the time that *Brokeback Mountain* took place, and it has forced me to look at my life and what it has meant and how it has affected others.

I knew I was different from others at a young age, too young to even know what sex was. I was raised in a strict Catholic family; sex was never talked about. Sad to say, I learned everything I know about sex through magazines and childhood friends. There was no manual on how to deal with your feelings back then. I fooled around with the neighbor boy for a few years while in high school. There was really no love or fireworks going off for us, just an outlet for sex. We were good friends to each other, but never really talked to each other in public. It was our secret. In my senior year, I started going to dances and drinking a lot. Guess it was my way of dealing with what was wrong with me. God, you can't imagine how I felt. I was so lost, wishing that I were normal like all my friends. The drinking helped me cope.

I met my wife at a dance. We hit it off right away. She liked my company and I hers. Again, the sex was really nothing to me, just an outlet for getting off. Most of the time, I had been drinking, and it wasn't a problem. It was easier for me to get the deed done. It sounds terrible, but that was the way I felt. I would go as far as to stay up late so I wouldn't have to have sex. She never complained; she just thought that, for me, sex wasn't really a big issue.

I had lived this life for six-and-a-half years when the movie *Making Love* came out. She and I went to see it. I was seeing my life on the screen. I remember the reaction in that theater when the two men first kissed. People were grossed out, even my wife. I was in awe that men really do this with each other. Even when I messed around in school with the neighbor boy, it was just mutual masturbation; we did go down on each other, but there was no kissing or closeness in it, just getting off.

After seeing the movie, I was in a state of mindlessness. I couldn't keep from thinking about it. My marriage really started to go downhill from there; I wanted something or someone to fill that longing. I distanced myself from my wife, and by now I had three little boys. I was mean to her and hateful. It got to the point that I didn't even want to be around her. The thought of her touching me, or even trying to get close to me, made me feel like shit. This went on for several months. I finally broke down and we had a long talk. I told her that seeing the movie had changed my whole outlook on life. I said that I couldn't cope with the lie anymore. I was gay.

You would have thought someone had put a gun to her head and pulled the trigger. She was devastated. At first, she thought it was a passing thing and that I would come back to my senses, but I told her I had been hiding these feelings all along and just did not know how to cope with them. She cried, and then the anger hit: she told me that our marriage was a big lie; how could I have done this to her and to our children? I tried to explain that I didn't do it intentionally; I was just trying to live a normal life as society expects of us. We tried to coexist together, but it wasn't working.

I was managing a convenience store at the time and met Richard, who worked at another store with the same company. The first time I saw him, I knew he was gay. I guess you could say I was the one who finally brought up the question about being gay. He said he was, but he also lived in the closet. He wasn't married, and we hit it off right away. We became good friends, talked about things and life. We started riding around together after work and just liked being around each other.

One day, we were at my house and my wife was at work; she was working the graveyard shift. I had put the boys to bed, and Richard and I were watching TV. In all the time that we had spent together, it was never anything to do with sex. We were sitting next to each other, and Richard leaned over and kissed me on the cheek. Wow, that surprised me! I really hadn't thought of having sex with him; I just enjoyed his company and having someone to talk to. Well, it got to heavy kissing and we moved to the bedroom. It seemed everything was going well, and then I thought, this isn't what I want from him. I didn't see us as being lovers. I wasn't attracted to him sexually. I stopped and explained to him how I felt. Damn, he understood, and we got up and went back into the living room. We talked for hours, and he decided it was time I went to a gay bar.

God, I remember that first time in a gay bar. I was in heaven, seeing all of the men so free and relaxed with each other—dancing together, kissing, cuddling, and having a good time!

Well, I finally got the courage to go by myself. I met a few guys and finally had sex, but it was nothing more than sex.

My marriage had come to an end; we both finally realized that it wasn't working. She told me that she was letting go of her best friend and was going to have a hard time coping. I moved out to a town five miles from where we had lived.

Christmas came around, and she asked if I could come by and help her assemble some of the gifts for the boys. As we were getting stuff ready, she was becoming more frustrated and finally broke down and started crying. She told me that she didn't know how to deal with this. She was so lost and had no one to turn to or talk to. I realized then what I had done to her and my family. I said I would be there anytime she needed help or to talk. She asked me to come back, but I said I just couldn't live that way anymore.

I met my Jack at a bar not too long after that. He was my cowboy dream! We hit it off the moment our eyes connected across the room. I was standing alone, enjoying a beer, and he came over to me and asked if I wanted to come over to his table with his friends. I said okay. Damn, I couldn't believe he had asked me. We danced, joked around, and had a good time. He asked if I wanted to go to his place for a drink; I said okay. We were up all night talking about family, friends, and what we wanted in life. I wanted to jump his bones so bad, but we parted with a good night kiss, and he gave me his phone number.

I called him the next day, and we talked for hours. I remember my phone bill was sky high. We went out the following weekend and had a great time together—still no sex. The following weekend, I arrived ready to go out, and he had dinner ready. He had made stuffed pork chops. Damn, the man could cook, too! He asked if I wouldn't mind staying at the apartment. I said, "Sure, we don't have to go out."

That was the first time we made love, and I have never in my life felt so connected to a person as I did with him. We knew each other's every move and action. That whole weekend was so right. I finally told him that I thought I was falling in love with him; he said he felt the same way. It was so awesome! I moved into his apartment a few days later.

In the meantime, my ex was going through a lot herself. She got to the point that she couldn't cope with things. She dropped the boys off at my parents' and said she needed to get away for awhile. I made arrangements to put the boys in day care and move them in with us. I was so scared that my love was going to tell me that there's no way he was going to have that. But I was wrong. We didn't see my ex for almost a year. She disappeared. Finally, she came back and I asked her what she was going to do about the boys. She said she wasn't ready to take care of them yet. I let it go a few more months and then asked her for custody. She asked why, and I said that they were already settled with us, and it would not be a good idea to take them out of their new home. She agreed and gave me custody.

That was twenty-three years ago. We now have a little granddaughter who is the light of our lives. My Jack has loved me unconditionally for all these years.

Back in 1999, he suffered a heart attack and underwent bypass surgery. God, I thought I was going to lose him. What was I going to do without him? Everything turned out fine. He's doing great now, and life is good. When he was in the hospital and I rushed to see him, my middle son was with me. When we left later that night, my son told me that when he saw the way we looked at each other, my Jack and me, for the first time he realized how deeply I felt for this man. Through the years we have never really showed any affection in front of the boys. They consider him another dad.

So many people have been hurt because of me. I'm glad that the younger generation has accepted gays as part of the norm. All of our sons are straight. We joke that we don't know where we went wrong.

Brokeback Mountain has brought up so many memories. It has refreshed my love for my Jack. I don't know what or where I'd be without him.

My ex-wife and I are still good friends. The boys tell me that she still is in love with me, but she's glad that I'm happy. She was remarried for about ten years, but she's since divorced.

Thanks to *Brokeback Mountain* I've had a chance to look back and see my life again. It was hard going at first. I thought I would never be happy. But things happen, sometimes for a reason. I never regret anything and never will—because I have my Jack, and life couldn't be any better!

Jim Titzman, 48, works in sales and lives with his life partner, Gabby, in Pleasanton, Texas. He posts under the screen name of jt44.

16 Don't Let this Happen to You

—exennis

I am thirty-six. I spent three-quarters of my life living like Ennis, filled with a crippling paranoia and fear from my earliest memories. Even when I was seven or eight, I knew something was "wrong" with me. At that age, I didn't even know what that something was, but I instinctively knew that I had to hide it at all costs. I shudder to think what psychological damage that does to a child. As I got older (and particularly as a teenager, the cruelest age group), I would constantly monitor my every movement and every word, afraid that someone might guess I was gay. I was good at it. No one ever guessed.

I went to an all-boys boarding school in England. In my final two years (when I was sixteen/seventeen), I had an intense but platonic relationship with a guy in my year. He was the stereotypical Mr. Popularity: incredibly good-looking, popular with students and staff, sporty, captain of the rugby team, etc. I was not unpopular, or even geeky, but I was the studious, pensive type in a school that placed a premium on sporting prowess. We'd been at the school for three years and barely spoken to each other. Suddenly one day, without warning or explanation, he started coming on to me.

He searched me out during free periods and wanted to talk about "deep" things, or at least what passes for deep when you are a teenager. I was completely baffled and disoriented by the attention, but also flattered. I kept asking myself why he chose me. He admitted that his own friends were beginning to ask him about our friendship. Slowly, things got more intense. Our bedrooms were at opposite ends of the school, a big, neo-Gothic pile from the 1830s; and we would creep down the corridors at night to each other's rooms, trying to avoid the night watchman. Our conversations would last deep into the night. We would pick each other up every morning before heading for the communal showers. If you think Jack had difficulty not looking at Ennis when he was washing, imagine what difficulty I had in those showers! My grades started to suffer; I began falling asleep in class. I was falling in love. It remained platonic, although he sometimes stroked my cheek or even my bum. I was confused, but so happy.

Then, two years later and just before we sat for our final exams, he suddenly dropped me without any explanation. I was devastated. I messed up my A-Level exams, which are vital for going to university. I went off the rails and started drinking heavily. I was beginning to realize, after a lifetime of denial, that my homosexuality was not just a phase; I was stuck with it and . . . stuck with living in the closet like Ennis, forever. This led to some dark moments. Over a period of years, I eventually got my life back in order, but it was a close shave. To this day, it is the only time in my life that I have lost it.

The securest prisons are those we create for ourselves.

I had seven girlfriends. The last one lasted for three years. We lived together and even talked about marriage. I was never unfaithful, but all the time I knew I was gay.

Eventually, I moved to another country and finally got what I needed, though still in absolute, ironclad privacy. Nobody knew about my double life. I never gave any personal information, or even my name, to the strangers with whom I slept. However, as I approached my late twenties, I sensed that I couldn't keep going on like this. I was going insane. Keeping up the pretense was beginning to wear me out, and most of my life was still stretching out in front of me. I finally cracked and started telling my closest friends. The first time was the hardest. I was shaking so hard and my teeth were clattering so loudly, my friend was worried I had a fever. It got slightly easier with each new person I told.

I started coming out of the closet at twenty-seven. I was nervous about telling my friend Mike because I wasn't sure how he would react, and he was the first male I had decided to tell. On the day I finally plucked up the courage to say it, we had already been best friends for four years. At first, he responded with silence. My heart sank, and I regretted saying anything. Then he said something that stunned me. He reacted in a way that hadn't even occurred to me—and I thought I had played through every possible reaction in my head beforehand. He said, "I thought we were friends. Why didn't you tell me before?" It had simply never occurred to me that my friends, far from being upset that I was gay, might actually be upset that I had chosen not to tell them.

When *Brokeback Mountain* opened here, I told Mike I wanted him to see it. While it wouldn't excuse what I did as a closet case, it might at least explain things a bit. He loved the film. He didn't just say he liked it, which I had expected him to say; he spent ages talking about it afterwards. His reaction is a testament to the power of *Brokeback Mountain* as a positive force for change.

The thought struck me after my second viewing, after I'd pulled myself together again—is this what mainstream love stories or tragedies feel like for heterosexuals? My whole life I've never really watched them because they left me pretty cold. Of course I responded to them intellectually. I understood why they were sad and why the people around me were crying, but emotionally, I was indifferent. I always chalked it up to not being an emotional person. Then *Brokeback Mountain* happened.

So, here I am today. I'm now half out of the closet, with a wonderful boyfriend of nine years. However, if he does something affectionate in public, my immediate instinct is still to shrink back in horror. I'm so ashamed of that. He understands why, but it must hurt him so much inside.

My closest friends know. My work colleagues don't. My family certainly doesn't. Every time I even think about telling my family, I am hit with waves of nausea, even dizziness. If I had seen *Brokeback Mountain* ten years ago, I can't imagine what effect it might have had on me. It might have been enough to tip me over the edge. Seeing it now has given me a massive boost of confidence and reassurance that I made the right decision to start coming out of the closet. The film means different things to different people, but for me it has one core message, which it delivers loud and clear: Look at Ennis; don't let this happen to you.

Purely as a result of this film, I'm beginning to wonder for the first time whether I now have enough courage to tell my family, or at least my sisters—hey, it's a start! If I do tell them, it will be because of this film, and this film alone.

Antony, 36, is a UK-based former journalist who works in the political arena as a speechwriter. He shares his life with his boyfriend and their dog. He posts under the name exennis.

...Ennis felt he was in a slow—motion, but headlong, irreversible fall.

17   Poems Inspired by the Film

The power of Brokeback Mountain *affected viewers in many ways. For many on the Forum it inspired the creativity on display below in these poems.*

Two Came Together

–Lancelot Price

Once in high summer
Two came together in love
And never left it

What the Tree Saw

–B73

It was nobody's business but theirs and yet
Above, standing sentinel a tree
Took in, along with sunlight
The radiance of an arm, a leg
Embracing madly the other
One, sheen of flank and thigh
Dark hair, light, bodies twisting
A vow, a threat, a promise
Of love beyond love's own tired meaning.

They imagined themselves invisible yet
Sighing as they did the boughs
In the wind watched, trembling as they did
The branches longed, to embrace too
The embrace upon the pine's own scattered needles.

Summer ended. Years passed.
A tree cut down, firewood
But within the ring from '63
Glowed there, the memory
Of a love long past, an afterimage
Like the sun behind the clouds behind closed eyes.

Jack Haiku

–Catalina

Teasing a smile
From a new friend's lips
Wine of the gods

Ennis Haiku

—Catalina

One man an island
Alone in a sea
Its water is fear

Love Wore a Black Hat

—B73

Love rode up in a black hat
Black truck beat up dustcloud
Like a twister; steps out
Long and lean as electric wire

Love rode up in a black hat
Shook my hand like a salesman
Sell me somethin' I don't need
Handshake sealed the deal right off

Love wore hisself a black hat
Set just so over cool drink cool blue eyes
You could drown in; dare to jump
Off that cliff to the center of nowhere

Last one in.

Hell drove away in a black hat
Drove away my guts turned
Inside out; guts upon dead pavement
Alleyway no shelter to that bitter dust

Rodeo

—B73

Gonna rope me a bronco
That one, over there
Got a low startle point but
I'm a bullrider, yes I am

Nervous young stallion
With tender brown eyes
Eyes like the mare that
Done throwed me; this one won't

Hold on for dear life
Ride that ride hard
A buckle for this one
Giddap! I ain't throwed yet

No one shot thing here, no
I'll chomp at the bit
But I'll gentle you down
And soothe you; stay now, sweet bronc

Gentle now, calm-like
It's all right; come here
My poor worried sweetheart
Ain't nobody's business, but ours

But who'm I foolin?
I'm the rider got rode
And you are the champion
I ain't buckin'; boy, you win the prize

Sacred

–bcatjr

Skittish colt you are
Came to me this sacred night
My hand to tame you

We Walked in Wind

–Lancelot Price

we walked in wind, free like waves in the grass of the plains as far as we could see.
hand in hand, skin to skin, skin to sky, saying no words, and none to say
words against
us.
two in one soul, one wind, one world.

Jack, Thinking of Ennis

–NotBastet

My quiet cowboy,
Ennis—my only. Let me
rescue you, love you.

Ennis, Thinking of Jack

–NotBastet

Open, free, loving.
Always dreaming. So different.
Jack—precious, shining star.

No Little Thing

—royandronnie

It's all right.
No. It isn't.
Look into my eyes. I'm in love with you.
I can't meet your eyes. Everything I feel for you is there.
Let me kiss you. Let me fold you into my arms.
It's wrong. It's wrong to want this.
Let me draw you down. Let me feel your weight on me.
I'm afraid of you. I'm afraid of myself.
Run your hands over me. I long for your touch.
I'm not queer. I don't want to be queer.
I will care for you. I will protect you.
I'm in agony. I can't breathe. You're touching me so gently.
It feels so right.
Why does it feel so right?
Because it is right.
Because it is right.
I want you more than I've ever wanted anything.
I want you more than I've ever wanted anything.
You are so strong. Make me yours always.
I am so weak. Make me yours always.
It's nobody's business but ours.
I don't care if it is queer.
I will touch and taste every inch of your body.
Cover my mouth with your own. Teach me how to kiss you.
I will set you free.
Set me free.
I have wanted this all my life.
At last. At last I know what I really want.
I want you.
I want you.
Come home.
I am home.
Soulmate.
Beloved.
It's all right.

Fear

−NotBastet

Strangers not for long.
Brokeback—soul mates united.
Kept apart by fear

Coupling

−Catalina

Electric like the lightning
Crashing on the peaks
Unexpected home

Screen Door

−B73

Screen door glass so clear that day
No streak or print to mar it
Cleaned it only yesterday
I'm a good wife, yes I am

Screen door glass so clean and bright
Just like it weren't there
A clear view right down to the steps
Nothin' 'tween me and them

Glass was dirty after all
Fogged with heartbreak's exhalation
Stained forever by betrayal
Never to be clean again

Starlight

—Cynical21

Stars in the night pale
before the starlight in his eyes.
Jack is smiling.

This Moment

—Plumtree11

Give me your hand, friend,
Let us relive this moment.
Never enough time.

America the Beautiful

—B73

<u>I. King of the Road</u>

I'm a man of means, by all means! But still
I'm king of the road, yes, this road! And will
By all means find somehow the means now ta be
The Lord of America; I am its king!

King of a cow and calf type operation
No more will it be such a bitch situation
I have in my hand a note he done scrawl
"Divorce is now final"; translation? "I call!"

"I call ta ya cowboy, come take me away
"We'll lick old man Twist's goddam ranch into shape!
"We'll build us a cabin, built only for two
"A sweet life at last now, just me and just you!"

Now free from a jail of waiting and tears
Now free from the yearning of all the long years
I'm free of ya, Brokeback, you bitter old man
No road will be closed now; I'm king of this land!

II. Crown of Thorns

I'm a man of means, by no means, I swear
I'm king of the road yes, the road ta nowhere
A sweet life behind me, and nothing ahead
America's empty, the land dry and dead

Ain't nowhere now here for all that I am
Ain't nowhere for me ta live a whole man
And bitter's the dust of a dream that done died
But dreams are for angels; and angels, they lie

Oh you're real sorry, real sorry, I'm sure
The girls and the roundup, oh ain't you so pure?
An upstanding citizen, and no you ain't queer
Trade glory for duty, trade lovin' for fear

Drive yonder now, cowboy, go down t' the south
Perhaps you can wash out the dust from your mouth
And maybe pretend for a minute or two
That the best thing about you had said "Jack, I do."

Return to Sender

–B73

Hell yes I been to Mexico
That a fuckin' problem
Dirty suckerpunch to the gut
You got me back for that one
I keep you on a short leash, Jack?
I don't know how bad it gets?

I wish I knew how to quit you too
I can't stand this anymore

Well maybe it be over now
Dust of irrigation ditch so chokin'
I guess I wasn't much fun anyhow
Guess nothin' was good enough for you, bud

But dry dust in my throat ain't shit
Compared to that dry desert of four years
Jack Pine Creek November 7th?
Don't leave me in that desert ever again, never again

See if I care

–magicmountain

OK so you don't need me the same
Not like my need
See if I care

You don't need my touch
My laughing
Eyes on you
See if I care

You don't need
my breathing in your ear
Not quite swallowing
all those words of love
See if I care

You don't need
my bitter parting kiss
You have turned around already
See if I care
I had to turn around

Over days and nights
sucking in your pain
Your whispering roared in my ears
It crumpled my insides
Just now I need to keep upright
Wade through the undertow to shore
Then I will retch it all out
and all the light and joy of you!

OK so you don't need me the same
(Sucking in your pain)
Not like my need

You don't need my touch
(Over days and nights)
My laughing
Eyes on you
(It crumpled my insides)

You don't need
my breathing in your ear
(Your whispering roared in my ears)
Not quite swallowing
all those words of love
(Then I will retch it all out)

You don't need
my bitter parting kiss
(Just now I need to keep upright)
You have turned around already
(Wade through the undertow to shore)

You don't need
(all the light and joy of you!)
See if I care

Untitled
-bcatjr

I stood there.
A pillar of strength.
So I thought.
I could do this, I could hold off the thing that meant the world to me.
Make it stand tall somewhere else, instead of beside me.
Where he belonged.

I was scarred.
Blackened.
But time took care of that.
It stripped me bare.
Took away my coloring and left me gray.
Standing tall, naked and all alone.

Waiting
-Cynical21

Your fire is cold, your music lost,
I breathe you, dream you,
and wait to die.

Lullaby
-B73

Where I'm at now you can't see me
Way up high among the hazy blue
And you can't know that I am watching
In the sweet cool dream forever

Up here in the sweet forever I can read your mind
The mind you never deigned to share with me
It's funny how I know you better now
Since the world and I had parted company

If I could, I'd comfort you and tell you it's all right
I'd sing the song that you once sung to me
But instead I'll watch you, see you safe
In the sweet cool dream forever

Ennis, being lonesome don't mend matters
And the whisky ain't much help now neither
But each new wrinkle, each grey hair I cherish
In the sweet cool dream forever

I heard your whispered vow to me
I heard your silent prayer
I know more than you did what you meant
When you said Jack I swear

Will you ever look up at the stars again
And wonder what it's like up there
If you do, perhaps you'll see me
In the sweet cool dream forever

See me waiting for you here
In the sweet cool dream forever

The Columbine Lament

–Plumtree11

In the meadow on high
We would smell grass and pine
And embraced we would lie
In the wild columbine.

Scalding tears of guilt;
Never said "You are mine",
And my lover got killed
In the wild columbine.

Weary life of regret
I will drown in wine,
For my lover is dead
In the wild columbine.

Soul wilted and bled,
Of my death warning sign,
For my lover's long dead
In the wild columbine.

I will never forget
Till my last day's decline
Smell of grass when we met
In the wild columbine.

Two Shirts

–Plumtree11

Remember these shirts?
That smell of grass and mountain air
Lingering no more.

Aging Ennis Haiku

–Whiplash

Your face a memory
Our threadbare sleeve entwined
Come home to me now

Soiled

–planetgal471

I wash my sheets every single week.
I used to wash them every couple months.
They were just as spunk-filled then.
Now, the smell suffocates me,
Smelling like my times with him.
Once, I washed them two days in a row;
I didn't think I'd got the smell out.
Then I knew the smell was in my nose,
The smell of anguish long-laden,
The smell of knowledge that this,
This was my life.
This was to be my life forever.
This was always the future I had in mind,
But I found, now that I had it,
Somewhere inside I had harbored
Some secret knowledge that
the world would change--
Or I would--
Or he would.

I don't think I knew anything of hope
Until I felt its absence

Widower

–Sheera

I cain't help but think—
folks might call me a widower,
if they'd want a word for me other'n
fairy or fag—
but they'd be wrong,
though you was the one that died.

'Cause I see now,
missin' you with everythin' I got,
and sayin' goodbye to you ever' second
since I read that word like dyin',

That you was the one,
all this time,
who was the widow

of a man
living.

"Jack, I swear—"

Pentecost

–B73

Wings brush the desert of my front door
The angel Gabriel, halo of golden fire
Hat in hand where his mighty sword should be

He come in and sit a spell, have a cup of coffee, woncha?
Piece of cherry cake? And as he fought
The Devil at my table, I did not have to ask:

Have you seen him sleeping?
Have you seen the lashes crost his pale cheek
A little boy, dreaming cowboy dreams

Did you tuck him in with care?
Palm of your hand brush back his hair
let him know it's all right, it's all right

Did you know his deepest dream?
Did he let you know what he could not tell me?
But I knew, I knew my boy, he didn't need to say

Did you know the child within the man?
The child what still is here, always. I kept his room
Like it was when he was a boy; you can go up there, if you want

The angel come back down, wings folded 'neath his arm
My boy with you always, Gabriel, in your care
Come back and see us again sometime

Regrets for Never Were

—Cynical21

How is it that I never knew,
Through all the lonely years ahead,
The things that I would mourn the most
Were all the words we never said?

Grieving still for vows unkept,
And all the music left unplayed,
With tears unwept that flood the soul
For promises we never made.

When efforts to recall your smile
Call up a stranger's face instead,
When memory fails and vision pales,
I'll still regret those words unsaid.

As time winds down and days grow short
And evening falls with vespers rung,
My tears well up and fill my heart
With all the songs we left unsung.

Drowned in the silence of your eyes,
As you deigned to follow where I lead,
The sadness lingers in my heart,
Still haunted by those words unsaid.

.And when my last mistake is made
In the place where lost illusions stir,
I'll mourn the chances left untaken
And all the dreams that never were.

Spiritual

–Sheera

It is what it is,
and we are what we are

We are all we can ever be,
all we will never be

In the slip-sliding loops of time,
I found your hand
And in the rushes of tomorrow's dream,
You found mine

They fit together,
speaking all the words
we are too afraid to say
Inextricably intertwined

Your death
was the beginning
of my understanding

I left pieces of me
on the road
…for you to find

Is there anything more than darkness,
at the end of our journey?
Can you lead me there?
Misfortunate carries a heavy price, wisdom

My name
was the final word you said to me
and I just wanted to tell you, that it is yours
to keep

Because this is all I can be,
and you are all I ever wanted to be

The Open Space

–TaoOfMeow

Draw me a picture, tell me a lie,
paint it with stars on a midnight sky.
Send me a signal, show me the way
back down the road to our yesterday.
The place once safe is ours no more...

Don't look...turn away, just shut the door.
The life you live, the company you keep
can't soothe your soul as you quietly weep.

A stoic existence, ever-unchanging,
but with loss finds itself rearranging
and becoming the very thing that you fear.
The loneliness that whispers into your ear:
"I *know* what you are...you can't ever hide
the truth that dwells within, deep inside.
You had your chance, and now it's too late
to pluck that joy from the jaws of fate."

True, it's too true...and you soon realize
that the man that you would canonize,
who only knew hope as a fragile thing
(a promise held aloft on a butterfly's wing)
was as frightened as you. Where would he be
if you had never met? Different destiny?
What's done is done—you can't go back
to find the courage you currently lack.

But in your dreams struck bright with pleasure
lives a passion so deep it can't be measured
by any earthly instrument known to man.
This all must fit in some greater plan.
An unbroken wheel, no beginning or end
that might help you find each other again.
You gaze through the window to the open road
where so many promises once beckoned and glowed.

Man should shape life not with words but deeds;
tend the blessed earth for the salvation he needs.
But the stark sere beauty of that unforgiving plain
would never bear fruit. What you sought to gain
only grew in his arms. How could it be wrong
when your heart would fill overflowing with song
at the very sight of your lover's warm stare?
So you offer that ghost a silent prayer:

I'll draw me that picture...tell truth and not lie.
Paint it in rainbows on a brilliant blue sky.
You'll send me a signal, you'll show me the way
back over the mountain to a happier day.
That place, so safe, will be ours once more.
It's alright...I'll wait, just a little bit more.
This life I still live, so your memory I'll keep.
I love you, I miss you...and I'll see you in my sleep.

Confessions of a Dream

–Sheera

"All that I lov'd
I lov'd alone."

I couldn't see
them,
who said they loved you.
Wife, kid, mama–
They must a, though.
Who wouldn't?

But did they kiss you
like I did
cold rain beatin' down on us?
Wet all over us,
soaked to our bones

but happy.

Because misery with you
always was better'n
happiness with anyone else.

When I'm dreamin' I see
you sayin' my name
over and over again.

Sometimes like the last time.
that last time you spoke afore
you were gone.

Like it better, though, when it's
like those other times.
Soft, quiet, prayer-like,
didn't even sound like a word.
"Ennis."

You always seemed to be thinkin'
If you said it enough when you thought I was asleep
that it'd save you.

Jack.

Sometimes I think lovin' you
Was the only kind a savin' I
knew how to do. And maybe
I'm the only one who really knew how.
Don't think no one else
Loved you like me.

Such a goddamned shame that
I never
said it to you,
other'n in my dreams.

If you can hear me, Jack—
I ain't afraid a savin' no more.
I'll keep on doin' it so long
As you see fit to keep comin'.

Love you, friend. Love
you to the bitter fuckin' end.

Anniversary

–B73

Forty-three years since the day I was new baptized
Forty-three years to the day you took my hand
Guided me to the mountain wellspring of oblivion
Our forty-third year anniversary, Jack
Thirty-nine years since the day I'm resurrected
Thirty-nine years to the day that you come back
Woken from the grave of a dry spell bleak and blasted
Our thirty-ninth year anniversary, Jack

Twenty-five years since the day I got a postcard
Twenty-five years to the day my heart done died
Wander like a ghost through the desert of oblivion
My twenty-fifth year anniversary, Jack

Dozy Haiku

–Whiplash

strong arms, moist warm breath
soft song memories held near
time, a rainbow, stops

Then there was forty feet of distance between them...

18 In a New Light

On the Forum, heterosexual men and women described how Brokeback Mountain *changed their attitudes toward gay people, love, and life.*

Weapon Against Ignorance

—Arethusa33

Everyone should have the opportunity to watch *Brokeback Mountain*. This masterpiece is a weapon against ignorance, intolerance, and the like. Rimbaud thought that poetry could change a life. I am one of those who believe that *Brokeback Mountain* can change a life.

Viviane is a bank employee who lives in Bordeaux, France.

Brother-in-law Was Loved

—MindyM

I am a fifty-six-year-old divorced woman. I have had such an incredible experience after watching *Brokeback Mountain* that I am still sorting out my emotions. I had low expectations going into the movie, due to all of the hoopla and negative comments. I was not prepared in any way for what happened to me as I watched it. I have never understood how people of the same sex could actually love each other like a man and a woman. I have tried in my life to come to terms with this, but without success. Then, as I was sitting there watching Ennis and Jack, it started to hit me with such power that I couldn't control it.

I was enthralled watching their love unfold on screen. The scenes in the tent were hard for me to watch and made me uncomfortable. But I made myself watch. I found myself wanting them to be together, watching how alive and animated and relaxed they were when they were with each other. I saw the unhappiness in their everyday lives as they struggled to be what society demanded. They came into my heart and mind, and I can't let go of them now. I cried through the last half hour of the movie. I completely broke down sobbing, and I couldn't stop.

I have been thinking about my former brother-in-law since I saw the movie. The last I heard of him was from my estranged husband in the fall of 1991, when he called and told me that Johnny was dying of AIDS in a hospice. I was devastated and cried myself to sleep that night. Johnny was only thirty-two at the time, and I had not seen him for about seven years. It was so difficult for all of us to accept when Johnny came out while he was in the Navy. I always sensed that he was an unhappy, tormented person, even when I first knew him in his early teens. But I didn't know why. So now I know.

I have peace of mind knowing that Johnny knew that he was always welcome in our home and that he was loved. We did not turn away from him, even though we did not understand him. It may sound silly, but I woke up early one morning this last weekend, and it came over me that Johnny was really happy with his partner. In fact, it was the happiest I had ever seen him, just like with Ennis and Jack. He could never have known that his escapades in West Hollywood would end up costing him his life. But I can remember him now, and I feel some peace knowing that he lived his life the way he wanted. He got to be his true self in a way that Ennis and Jack never could. He lived openly as a gay man, and I know that when he died this horrible death, at least he had realized what he had been so desperately searching for all those early years of his life.

That's what *Brokeback Mountain* did for me. I know how beautiful love between two men can be. I have to stop now, because I am crying and I am overcome with my emotions.

Changing Hearts

—Poohbunn

At times, I feel strong enough to take a stand to stop creating more Jacks and Ennises, men who can't express their love freely. I know this is the most important way the movie affected me. I'm not going to remain silent in the face of this horrible bigotry anymore.

I hope the Brokeback effect will spread even further with the DVD out. I bought extra copies as loaners for my friends who haven't seen it. Even if one heart is changed, and one mind opened, it will have been worth it.

Here's a funny thing I've noticed these past few days: my husband says "tell you what" several times a day. Now I don't even know at this point whether he's always done this (shame on me for my married complacency) or whether it's a result of seeing *Brokeback Mountain* last week.

Another opportunity for Brokeback speech came up this past weekend while we were away in the mountains (having, yes, a Brokeback vacation). It's not the season now for snow, but heavy clouds, low temperatures, and a chilly forecast combined to give me a chance to say, "Gonna snow tonight for sure." How bloody pleased with myself I was!

My Good Man

—GGirl

Incidentally, my reluctant Brokaholic hubby showed his colors during our mountain adventure. This is a man who'd no sooner verbally acknowledge the presence of a gay couple than fly to the moon. It doesn't need attention drawn to it. And, of course, there's the fairly genuine irrelevance it has to his life. So there we were, just entering the high country, pulled over to a rest stop on the highway.

The first people we see are a gay couple and the "mother-in-law," clearly en route to the same location as we were. (Brokeback vacation? Highly likely!) His nibs straightaway mentions their "gayness" and points out in gormless fashion, "The mother doesn't seem to be bothered; that's good." After a quiet chuckle, I reminded him that part of her job description as a mother is to want happiness and good health for her boy—which he clearly had both of, in spades.

Let me say right now that this change in my good man is something, and can only be a result of *Brokeback Mountain*. He went on to mention the film several times over four days, and always in a positive way. This is a man who forgets what movies are about five minutes after seeing them, even the ones he likes. He called me into the living room of our cabin at one point, very excitedly, with "Quick, *Brokeback Mountain* is on TV." On another day, we passed through a gorgeous little high country town, just starting to be gentrified (or yuppified, if you like). There was an old, derelict, but beautiful art deco cinema there, and he said, "We could buy it, restore it, and screen nothing but *Brokeback Mountain*." Of course, this was said with a smirk, but just the fact that it entered his head is kind of amazing. It was my sad duty to tell him we'd end up a pair of freaky old Rocky Horror types and our kids would divorce us at age fifteen.

GGirl is from the Deep South and vacations as much as possible with her family in the mountains.

New Color

—sarah

I was so touched, mesmerized, bowled over, and dumbstruck over the love scenes: it is like seeing a color I've never before experienced, as if love itself has been reinvented. And yet, there is an absolute reverence for, and protectiveness towards, what these two men are experiencing, and respect for their privacy and God-given feelings for one another. So it is not a voyeuristic thing, but a savoring of the art, beauty, and spirituality that make up physical love on this level.

Sarah Murray, a 49-year-old sociology professor from New Jersey, is married with three children and loves the arts and literature. She posts using the name Sarah.

Gay Reality

—Jenny

It was reading in the Forum here that really brought home to me the fact that, because we internalize these rigid rules for male behavior, we set up a crippling series of obstacles for gay guys at every point in the journey towards a fully loving relationship: from acknowledging who you are and what you want, to acting on it, to finding and holding on to a particular person, and finally to functioning as a couple just as entitled to the acknowledgement and acceptance from your society as any other. I don't know whether anyone, gay or straight, can really say what gayness would look and feel like if those boundaries came down, nor what non-sexual relationships between men would be like.

I would have said that I was sympathetic to gays and lesbians, supportive of gay rights, and comfortable with my gay friends before I ever saw *Brokeback Mountain*. That's all true. But after I saw it and came to this Forum and read these discussions, I realized how blind I really was to the reality of being gay, even now. I'm not a deeply religious woman, and I'm not Christian, but I would say that God has granted me the grace to better understand what I thought I already knew.

A former mental health clinician, book reviewer and Annie Proulx fan, Jenny is married and lives in New Jersey.

Speaking Up For Gays

—mcnell1120

A few weeks ago, a co-worker whom I thought was a good, well-rounded person came up to me and said, "How disgusting that you have those two guys on your screensaver [Jake Gyllenhaal and Heath Ledger as Jack and Ennis]—what do you see in them? People need to be in a state of grace!" I went off on her, and she came back and kind of apologized in her own way a couple of days later. Well, I let that one go: no use getting all bent out of shape over one ignorant person, I said to myself.

I went outside to have a cigarette (I'm an ex-smoker and need a fix every now and then). Being outside with a few other gals, her included, I made a comment about my favorite actor, Jake Gyllenhaal. I didn't even mention *Brokeback Mountain*. She then goes on and on about the "gays" as everyone stood there kind of laughing but not sure of the situation, all looking at me. I inhaled one last time from my cigarette, slammed it down on the pavement and said, "You know, every time you open your mouth and spit out those ignorant comments to me, I lose my respect for you!" Wow, did I get a look! I ran back upstairs to my little hole in the ground they call a cubicle and felt like a mouse being chased by an angry cat. I felt alone and sad.

Never in my life have I felt so compelled to stick up for gay people. I have always been on "your" side, but I never felt it was my place to say anything. How wrong I was to think that. With all my gay buddies I've had over the years, we never really talked about stuff like this bothering us. They kept it to themselves, and I did too. It wasn't until this movie came along that I just had to jump in the cold water and face the tide. Right now, I'd rather swim with live sharks.

Nellie, a 40-year-old married mother of two from Chicago, is an insurance adjuster who loves painting and photography. She posts under the name Mcnell1220.

Unsuspected Prejudices

—JanieG

Like most people here, I wanted to talk about *Brokeback Mountain* all the time, mainly because I wanted friends to share in how I was feeling and have this wonderful experience for themselves. So imagine how I felt when I met with a solid wall of resistance. People I've known and liked for years revealed themselves to be narrow-minded bigots with the sort of prejudices I never suspected. It made me realize, in a tiny way, the problems gay people cope with every day of their lives.

Janie, 60, is a retired geography teacher who lives in the northwest of England with her husband.

Connection to Masculine Pain

—quijote

For me, there is a simple explanation for why there is little talk of Alma and Lureen. I'm a straight woman raised in a patriarchal-to-the-extreme household. I can tell you their suffering is par for the course. We know it; we feel it; and we live it in one way or another every day of our lives. We know more than we care to about emotionally unavailable or cheating men. Although I believe that without the suffering of the families—mother, daughters, wives—that this movie would not have the impact that it does and would not be the work of art that it is, the fact remains that we already know about the women. We are laid low by this movie because we finally can connect to masculine pain. Because we have not had occasion to see two men in a timeless romance, they are our focus in this movie.

When Jack says that the truth is that he misses Ennis so bad he can hardly stand it, Jake Gyllenhaal made this movie so real and human that I will never see men, especially gay men, the same, ever. They became something new, something fully human. I never knew I was missing anything. I thought I had empathy. I had nothing.

Since I now fully identify with and connect with the men, they are telling my story as well as the women's. The two men also have equal power, and so we as women are drawn to them to tell our story in a way never told before by women characters. It is a powerful thing for us to have our hearts rendered anew in male bodies. I think that's why the men are so stunning.

quijote is a 49-year-old soccer mom and lawyer who lives with her two daughters in the southern United States.

New Awareness

—Michelle Tisseyre

I'm just back from seeing it for the seventh time. The place was two-thirds full, all women, in ones and twos. I went alone and stayed till the end of the credits, along with a handful of others scattered about the theater. There was a sense of reverence about it.

I feel better now that I've seen the movie again. It was like seeing an old friend. Nothing can diminish its beauty or its profundity. Sitting there this afternoon among my sisters, many of them straight women like me, I was yet again reminded not only of how much this movie has changed people's lives, but of how much it has broadened and heightened our awareness of the invisible, vulnerable minority among us.

I am a straight woman with few gay acquaintances—none in my immediate family—only one childhood friend and just one other friend I made in my early twenties, before we moved on to different cities. I am progressive and have always supported gay rights on principle. But *Brokeback Mountain* was a revelation for what it made me feel, for what it made me share of the anguish and pain and fear and shame and love and longing and desire and loneliness and humiliation and injustice that gay men suffer throughout their lives. It got inside my head and my heart, and it changed me. The new awareness I have gained is part of me now, and of how I see the world. This is why it is such a monumental work. It's transformational. It speaks to the heart and nourishes the soul. It is not only memorable, but also unforgettable.

Michelle Tisseyre is a married 58-year-old novelist, translator, journalist, and activist from Montréal, Québec in Canada. She uses michelle *as her screen name.*

19 The Brokeback Miracle

—Robert Baxter

Reprinted with permission from the Courier-Post, Cherry Hill, N.J., a Gannett Company newspaper.

Brokeback Mountain hit me like a Mack truck. It ran right over my body and left tire tracks—indelible and permanent—on my soul. Overwhelmed, I set off on a journey, a difficult journey that took me up the mountain to rebirth and renewal. As I watched homophobia destroy Jack and Ennis, I was forced to face painful memories locked inside my heart. Suddenly, all the pain, all the hurt, and all the anger exploded. Every day, for more than a month, during long walks, I confronted long-suppressed memories and struggled to come to grips with the demons those memories freed.

My first memory, a happy one, stretches back to the age of five or six. I was holding my grandmother's hand as she introduced me to her cowboy pals, Bud and Manuel. From their scuffed leather boots to their weathered Stetsons, they looked like real men—lean, muscular, with big, calloused hands and strong faces, tanned by the sun. Bud owned a cattle ranch. Manuel was his foreman. They built barbed-wire fences and rode the range together on horseback. Later on, I realized they also shared a bed.

Bud and Manuel were gay cowboys, even though neither man would have known what "gay" meant sixty years ago. In those days, gay folk were called queers and homos. Nobody who knew Bud and Manuel would have dared ask if they were gay, but everyone sensed Bud belonged to Manuel. They were an inseparable pair, just like my grandmother's married friends.

I thought a lot about Bud and Manuel after viewing *Brokeback Mountain*. They are long gone, but I wish they were here to share their story with me. How did they forge a relationship in rural California in the 1940s?

I know all about the homophobia that existed in 1963, the year Jack met Ennis on *Brokeback Mountain*. I came out that same summer—not in rural Wyoming, but at a liberal California university.

Like Ennis, I kept telling myself, "I ain't queer." Finally, after years of tortured denial, I embraced what I am—gay. It was rough then. There were no support groups and no resources available to provide a helping hand as we struggled to accept our sexuality and overcome the hatred and self-loathing society heaped on us. Five of my close friends at Stanford, I later discovered, were also gay, but that was a subject we couldn't raise with each other until years later. We were too uptight and, I guess, ashamed. So we led our secret lives.

Three visual metaphors from *Brokeback Mountain* echo in the memories of every gay man who came out when Ennis and Jack were struggling to accept their love: the closet, the bloodied shirts, and the tire iron. Most gay men were wedged in closets so tight and airless we could barely breathe. We all had our bloodied shirts—the secrets and the pain and hurt we experienced. We all feared the tire iron that could strike suddenly and violently. My gay friends have been attacked with everything from broken bottles and baseball bats to rocks and ice picks.

A less than lethal version of the tire iron that killed Jack Twist hit me on a warm summer evening as I walked down Pine Street in Philadelphia. Suddenly, in the glow of twilight, a hate-filled face loomed in front of me. A fist smashed into my head. I sank to my knees, blood streaming onto my shirt. The gay-basher slunk away, a dark, mean figure. I was stunned by his blow, but also shocked by the sudden silence on a street filled with people. Nobody stopped—not a passerby or a person in a car. "Are gay people invisible?" I asked myself as I tried to staunch the blood. Staggering, I turned down a side street. Two gay guys sitting on a stoop took me in and cleaned me up.

When I got home, the phone rang. It was my parents. They must have sensed the danger from a long distance, but how could I tell them their son had just been attacked by a gay-basher?

This was yet another secret to lock up with all the others.

I was lucky. I survived. Three of my friends in graduate school did not. After years of painful rejection by his homophobic father, Joe swallowed a bottle of sleeping pills. They found his body on a deserted beach. David tried to hide who he was in a loveless marriage. It failed. He called his mother and told her he was going to kill himself. "Why not?" she replied before hanging up. He disemboweled himself with a steak knife. Ron was forced into an unhappy marriage by his father, a prominent evangelist. Unable to meet his father's expectations, he put a gun to his own chest and fired a shot through his heart, a final rebuke aimed at his heartless father.

Those deaths devastated me. Why were the bodies of these smart, talented, but tormented young men lowered into graves before their time? Little by little, I learned to hide those bloodied shirts in the closet stuffed with other painful memories. As Ennis del Mar says, "If you can't fix it . . . you got a stand it."

I locked away a lifetime of hate and persecution in an emotional tinderbox that ignited when I saw *Brokeback Mountain*. Suddenly, all the hurt exploded. I sobbed. Tears flowed, but they couldn't wash away the stains left by the deaths of my young friends and decades of hurt and secrets unshared.

Brokeback Mountain started me on a journey of self-healing. During my walks, I confronted many things I had long suppressed. Everything came spilling out. With the help of friends, I worked through it all. The journey was difficult. It was painful. I wouldn't trade that trip for anything. It has led me to self-understanding and self-acceptance. It has filled my soul and my body with a gentle inner peace I have never known. I call it the *Brokeback* miracle, a gift Annie Proulx and Ang Lee gave to me and to so many other people.

Brokeback Mountain also brought back another, happier memory. After his mother died, Bud showed up at our door. He said his mother wanted my mother to have her gold earrings. She has worn them for more than fifty years. Although she has probably never thought of those earrings as a gift from one mother of a gay son to another, I do. Last year, my mother lost one of the earrings. She was heartsick. A friend of mine called to console her. In the middle of their conversation, she told my mother what a loving son she has. "And you know all of his secrets, don't you?" my mother replied. A week later, she found her cherished golden earring. And now, thanks to *Brokeback Mountain*, her son has no more secrets to hide.

Robert Baxter, 66, is an award-winning journalist, arts critic and opera lover from Cherry Hill, New Jersey. He posts under the name of Tacitus.

20 Call Me "Jack Twist"

—Pierre

I found out about myself a long time ago when, in junior high school, I was strangely attracted to a kid in my seventh grade class. His shirt was ripped to shreds after a rough, recess, football game. For some reason, that whole day I would steal glances at him. Before long, I was fantasizing about him and other similar guys. I was twelve or thirteen at the time, and though what I was experiencing was new, I knew it wasn't "natural"; so I denied it—for years. I played my role and had school girlfriends. Guys would hit on me, but I'd act uninterested despite my curiosity.

Years passed; my father died. He had been the most important man in my life, and I came to realize I can only live for myself and not to the likings of any other person on this planet. If I am to be judged, it will be by my Lord; and no one else will judge me. Slowly, I started accepting myself. For two years, I explored a relationship with a boyfriend for whom I care even to this day. However, that wasn't meant to last, and eventually he left me for someone else. This broke my heart, and I swore it would be the last time I'd ever be hurt that much again. I was content with frivolous dates and occasional sex to meet my needs, and, though hopeful, I was not expecting a deeper connection. Then I met my Ennis.

One evening, a guy I met online asked if I wanted to meet and maybe have sex. He said he was straight, had a girlfriend, hadn't been with a guy, but was curious. It was one of those nights, and he was close enough. He seemed to have more to lose than I did. So I went that evening and met him. I had no idea he'd be so attractive in person—tall, muscular, Hispanic. I met him, and though it was a warm September night, I was shaking from being so nervous. We talked a little, but I was shy because I didn't want to say the wrong thing. I wanted to respect his wishes, and I didn't want anyone to feel uncomfortable. He didn't want to kiss or cuddle, just get the satisfaction, and that's it. We did have sex that night, and it was great. Once again, I didn't think it was anything lasting. I thought I would just hold on to the memory. What happened next shocked me: he contacted me again asking to hang out. I was more than happy to oblige.

Over time, we would grow together and grow closer. He'd share more of his dreams and personal life. He'd come to tell me that I wasn't his first, but I was his best. I'd tell him about my plans and my family. He would stay longer and take more privileges with me, becoming more comfortable. He'd tell me how he'd dream about me, that I was his fantasy—that still puts a smile on my face. He would come to hold me tight as we lay together, take showers with me, and be more playful and more open. He would look at me and even kiss me, no longer seeing any harm in it. I'd let him drive my car, which I don't let anyone do, and I helped him move to a new place. He showed concern about our connection, asking if I'd ever deny him. I doubt I ever could. He only told me once that his father would not approve of what he was doing. That was the most he ever talked about his family's opinion of what he was doing with me. Honestly, I never needed to know.

This carried on and, unbelievably, still does, for over three-and-a-half years. A couple of girlfriends came and passed. I got excited when the first girlfriend left the picture, only to find out that she wasn't the stumbling block to our progression. He did move away, but we still stay in contact and speak of meeting up. I would move if I thought it meant we could try. I'm still pushing forward with all my plans to be a success, as I'm sure he is, too. So, even if our relationship seems shallow and uneventful, he is still the best man I know. He has never lied to me, led me on, or tried to hurt me. I can't judge what he is. All I know is how I feel when I'm with him.

I loved rubbing his head while he lay next to me, kind of reaching up to hug him, glowing in his eagerness. He always put a smile on my face, and no one else mattered when I was with him.

This is probably as much as we'll ever have. I think, with how he's been raised, our connection cannot be explored as deeply as he can explore a connection with a woman. It used to kill me. I used to brush it aside as much as I could. Now, I think I've just come to live with it.

Though I'm not holding my breath for him, there is still is no comparison to the devotion he's shown me through the years.

When I saw *Brokeback*, I was in shock. I saw it all: my curiosity about this other guy, the haphazard manner in which we physically connect, the unspoken tenderness, the societal confines, our ignorance of each other's internal struggles, the hope, the rejection, the attempts at replacement, the pure joy in those fast-fading moments, the sorrow, and the sacrifice.

He doesn't even call me; he prefers to e-mail, just as Ennis never called Jack and only mailed postcards. I'm the dreamer, less concerned with what others have to say; and he's the traditional man, hardworking and reared to be straight. Nonetheless, we somehow knock together and fit. I couldn't put him out of my life if I wanted to, yet I know this affects how I view my intimacy with other men. I can maintain other more defined relationships, but I know they are different from this unspoken connection I have with my Ennis.

My last gift to him was a CD of a song I had sung. He has told me how much he loves it, that he listens to it every morning, and how he'd love to see me again. Somehow, his opinion becomes the one that matters the most. Just imagining every morning that I'm with him is enough to get me out of bed with a smile.

So call me "Jack Twist." I hope my Ennis (straight bastard!) and I will eventually find a time where we can explore this further, but until then, "If you can't fix it . . . you got a stand it."

Pierre, 26, is a manager from Brooklyn, New York.

Ennis wrote back, you bet.

21   And the Greatest of These Is Love

On the Forum there is a thread called "Christians who love Brokeback Mountain.*" Here viewers discuss how their religion influenced their thinking about the movie.*

Support Is Not Enough

—Linda Andrews

The message of the movie for me is to reinforce my political and social views. I have had gay friends all my life; my best friend and soul-sharer is gay. He and I have been there for each other through everything. I always thought my support for him and my other gay friends was enough. That support showed the world that I was open and supportive.

This movie has proven to me that this is not enough. It has shown me that I must be more vocal, more reactive to people's homophobic opinions, speaking out to let them know that that is not something I will let pass as I have in the past. It has enabled me to put myself and my feelings out there. It has given me bravery to announce to everyone I know, and those I don't, that this is something I feel strongly about. Let's get the message out that everyone is created equal in God's eyes. He loves no one more or less than others, because He created all of us.

Fifty-four-year-old Texas-based widow Linda Andrews owns a needlecraft shop and also serves as a moderator for the Dave Cullen Forum. She usees killersmom *as her screen name.*

A Holy Moment

—Alma

I just returned from my sixth and final theater viewing of *Brokeback Mountain*. When the last scene ended and the credits rolled and Ang Lee's name hit the screen, I was in streaming tears. I felt proud of each name that filled the black space, as if they were personal friends. But more than anything, I came away from this odyssey of in-depth exploration of one piece of art with a commitment to honor love wherever it may be found. I am ashamed of the way our culture—my heterosexual, religious culture—has perpetrated violence and shame on those who would love each other.

I come from conservative Christians. One thing some of them say about homosexuality is that you can have the orientation, but you can't act on it, or it will cause you to sin.

What this movie did for me is to show me that love and sex are so thoroughly entwined that you do damage to your soul to separate them. Seeing two men who were genuinely in love make love . . . well, it was a holy moment. I felt privileged to witness it.

And I'm honored to have been a part of what I think will be remembered as a turning point in how homosexuality is understood in America. This is the best kind of art: the kind that works on your soul until it is shaped into something new. There is no going back after that.

Julie, 45, is a married mother of five who lives in the Midwest and who is a professional writer and business owner. Alma *is the name she uses for her posts.*

Grandmother's Touching Email

—Robert Baxter

One of my friends, a devoutly religious grandmother, bought *Brokeback Mountain* at the local WalMart yesterday. After viewing it, she sent me a most touching e-mail which I will paste into this post. Like so many straight people, she had no idea how society has treated gay folk. It's simply not in her experience. Well, after seeing *Brokeback Mountain* for the first time three months ago, I started an intense e-mail exchange with her about homophobia and how it has affected my life. She knows now, and her reaction to the film shows it:

> *It has taken nearly two hours to regain my composure. I need to talk about this film. It is so beautiful, so perfect, so unbearably painful to watch. From the moment Jack drives away, for the first of many times, and Ennis crumples in the alley, the truths start coming at me, the ugly truths: the hatred that haunts their love, the lies they both must live, the relentless onward movement of a tragedy unfolding. Yeah, Ennis, "no reins on this one": not just the passion, but the whole situation. Oh, please, say yes, Ennis, when Jack suggests "the little cow and calf operation." Or say yes when the divorce is final, and there is a single moment of hope. Of course he won't say yes. This is a script, and without conflict it won't maintain momentum. Oh, but I don't want it to maintain momentum, on the screen or off. I want all the Jacks and all the Ennises to live their lives in love and peace. I want the wretched hatred that flames in the eyes of the boss and Jack's father to soften into acceptance and understanding. I want both of those beautiful boys and all the others like them to sit down at the table together and have a piece of mother's cherry cake. I want no bloody shirts in the closet. I want no closet at all. I want no reason to sob without comfort for two hours after watching a movie that reveals such excruciating pain that I feel raw and bleeding from exposure to it. That's what I want. Yes, that's what I want.*

Robert Baxter, 66, is an award-winning journalist, arts critic and opera lover from Cherry Hill, New Jersey. He posts under the name of Tacitus.

A change of attitude is happening not only among the Christian and heterosexual members of the Brokeback *audience, but also among gay people, whom we usually think of as a liberal segment of society.*

Won't Settle

—Jack Mangan

The single best part of this *Brokeback Mountain* journey, the part I hope will far outlast the novelty of having our own great work of art, is that it has stirred a quiescent multitude of rural, suburban, and downright country gay men out of their settled, passive, and ultimately suffocating hidey-holes.

Having been disrespected or ignored by our so-called gay community, we have scanned the horizons and found a bleak landscape. By and large, we have settled: some for abstinence, some for furtive bathroom encounters, some for sex with prostitutes, some for computer porn. Many of us have all but given up the quest for a mate.

The sad thing—and this perhaps applies most to the real senior division here, such as myself— is that this is the time of life when engagement with the community and a friend/love really signifies the passage to a dignified, rather than pathetic, old age. My cat is great company, but he can't bring me breakfast in bed on a day when the joints don't want to work.

Even sadder is that those of us who have reached advanced years have a wealth of experience and hope to pass on, if only anybody was listening or even thought that there was beauty and worth in aging. Most of a generation of talent, love, and experience was wiped out by AIDS. This new, vibrant, gay youth culture has no immediately identifiable mentors to whom to turn. Whether they know it or not, they need us, and they need us to be strong and confident and aware of our own worth. This is a generalization, but most of us have not been doing much more than sunning on a rock.

I can't speak for anyone but myself here, but being strong and authentic and forward-looking is a job that requires more fortitude than I can muster on my own, most days. And I thought I was pretty much just that, on my own.

I can see now that I underestimated you. You are out there. And you share common life experiences and common fears and joys and sorrows with me. I hope crying over, or celebrating, this film brings us together. I need to know that all of you are out there to move forward, and I really hope that some of us can become real friends, and most of all I hope I can find my complement out there, hiding on a ranch, or in a flat, or, best of all, on a beach in Hawaii.

It has been more than a decade since I slept in the arms of another man, largely by my own choice, for I will not settle for Mr. Right Now. I have worked too hard and paid too dearly to become the man I am to disrespect myself with one-night-stands or weekend flings, tempting though that might be. I am worth love.

And so are you all, brothers....

Jack Magnan, 63, now semi-retired after an eclectic career, lives in Punta Gorda, Florida. He posts under the name Jack.

Dignity, Not Humor, for Gays

—Dan

I'm not sure I'm representative of any big demographic, but *Brokeback Mountain* has had one striking impact on the way I perceive the culture around me lately. It really offends me to see pop culture icons and entertainers resorting to the old stereotypes of gays for humor. Most entertainers would stop dead in their tracks about jokes that stereotype women or African Americans. But with gays, that type of offensive stereotyping has never even been questioned until now.

Brokeback Mountain has put a universal, dignified, human face on gay humanity. People may be taking a while to admit that many families everywhere have members who are not straight, but *Brokeback Mountain* delivers the stunning lesson that individuals' collisions with their gayness is a matter of supreme seriousness, maybe tragedy, maybe even majesty, and that anyone who wants to make fun of it is seriously embarrassing him- or herself.

Men's Emotional Burden

—BenKing

I was shocked by the scene where Ennis coughs and vomits when Jack leaves him the first time. I was totally caught off guard when it happened. I expected Ennis to go on being his stoic self while Jack went off and cried alone. Instead, we are allowed to see something new in a major film: a guarded, defensive, tough man bearing an extreme emotional burden by himself. We see this again when Ennis fights with the truck driver in front of the bar, when he finds the shirts in Jack's closet, and, of course, in the closing scene.

These two characters endure so much for love. This movie isn't just about all love. It's what gay love was like and still is in some places. And it shows how men carry and hide this emotional burden.

Now the whole country is discussing relationships between people of the same sex more openly than ever before. If one didn't have any idea of what that's like, the movie shows it. The audience gets to see something that's been hidden from most people their whole lives. The fact that in this movie the men bear most of the emotional burden is grossly understated. Yes, the women get hurt—it's a tragedy, so all characters suffer—but they have some success despite their husbands. One remarries the local grocer and raises their kids, and the other runs her father's business. They're heterosexual: they have a place in life. They aren't killed or sentenced to a life of loneliness like Jack and Ennis. This movie is one of the first times we see, in a film or story set in America, men carrying the emotional burden all the way through to the sad end and gay characters that aren't goofy, campy, suffering from AIDS, or effeminate. They're complete and real.

Inspiration

—Lyle Palaski

I met a friend at a party a month after I'd seen *Brokeback Mountain* for the first time on November 5th, 2005. As usual, we discussed some movies we'd recently attended and then he asked me about "the Ang Lee film." I blurted out, "I can't get it out of my soul." Right then I knew that it had its hold on me, that my life wasn't ever going to be the same. For it was true: I could not let go of it. Even though during some long days I did not want to think about the movie, it was there in my mind, tugging at my heart, wanting to be let in. What could I do but succumb to it?

Over the weeks since I have seen the film and read the story and seen the film and read the story and listened to the music and seen the film—you get the idea—all I know is that I have been inspired.

I've been inspired to be creative by a great work of art. The best works of art inspire people, and *Brokeback Mountain* does that.

I myself was inspired to write poems.

To write stories.

To write song lyrics.

To write letters!

It made me interested in rodeos! (Really!)

It made me cry . . . and laugh.

It's made me want to sing and dance!

It's made me want to live again.

It's made me want to love again!

To have hope.

Why? I don't know, but it has changed my life and I am forever grateful.

I offer my limerick as one small proof of this inspiration:

I've come to know Ennis and Jack.
They've shown me a life that I lack.
Sometimes I resist,
But with a nice little twist
I could get all my BROKEn dreams BACK.

Lyle Palaski, 51, lives in West Hollywood, California, and temps in office work as he pursues his dream of being a writer. He posts using the name Mooska.

The First Lesson I Learned

—Nelson Caron

Brokeback has become something very precious, profound, life-changing, even sacred.

I thought I didn't need anyone in my life. A boyfriend, what a burden. Always having to decide what to eat, what to see, what to do. I ought to know, I've had two boyfriends with whom I lived. Then it punched me in the gut after my first viewing of December 21st: I had been lying to myself for years. I realized I needed to be loved, to be loved by a man I'd love back. I had forgotten the positive sides of living with someone. *Brokeback* woke me up. This was the first lesson I learned, and I know there are more coming my way.

Nelson Caron is 42, lives in Montréal, Québec, makes wonderful tiramisu, and works as a freelance analyst-programmer.

22 The Maker Makes

—Ironwood

I don't consider myself a religious person in the usual sense of that term. I do believe, however, that there are persons who cross our life-path and are placed there for a reason. Maybe it's what "the Maker makes." My *Brokeback* is a story of such a crossing.

I feel both fortunate and somewhat guilty that, through circumstances or fate, I somehow avoided taking into adulthood the self-hate carried as a burden by so many of my brothers and sisters. I did carry forth my secrets, and, without guidance, I got most of the other relationship lessons twisted up.

I've always known I was homosexual; however, like so many others my age (born in 1943), I had no positive words or concepts to allow for early self-acceptance or even full awareness. I was raised in a rural area. I got a heavy dose of guilt from my Italian Catholic family and four years of nun-taught Catholic high school. I remember the angst of confessing my one-handed, adolescent adventures and never really understanding why God would find my solo pleasure so offensive. Experimenting early, from the age of seven clear though college, I had a succession of sex-play partners, with the last and closest to adulthood being with R and lasting over four years. I did not know what it was other than to think, like both Ennis and Jack, "I ain't queer." I created a divide between sex and love that rivaled the width of a Wyoming river canyon! Sex was what I did with boys, and love was what I could only get from girls; or so I believed.

So, at twenty-three, I married. Sexually, I was functional in the relationship; I have two grown children. However, my heart was never fully in the function, which became more and more difficult and less and less frequent as years rolled by. My dear wife had undemanding sexual needs and we were—and still are—best friends. We shared child-rearing, and she was always supportive of my career as a counseling psychologist. I've said before that while I did not fall in love with her, we grew in love over twenty-four years of a successful relationship. Memories of R faded. Still, I used them—and other created fantasies—as fuel for sexual arousal both in the infrequent couplings of marriage and in a return to one-handed adventures. Never in my wildest dream did I consider the possibility of what Jack Twist called the "sweet life."

Emotionally, I stumbled though adulthood, while professionally helping others to patch up and repair their lives. My own needs took a back seat. I was unaware till later of just how tightly wrapped I had become, how habitual was the close-guardedness that concealed my attraction to men, how stunting this was to my own adult development and to my own sense of personal freedom, and how much energy was being wasted by self-denial and subterfuge. As years passed, the pressure increased, but I had neither hope nor dream of change. I loved my wife and kids. Well into my fourth decade, I could not conceive of growing old without the status quo.

Well, the Maker had other plans. In early 1990, I went for a training workshop in clinical hypnotherapy to the garden isle of Kauai in Hawaii. Truly the paradise of *South Pacific* and *Jurassic Park* fame and home to "Puff the Magic Dragon," Kauai was as far from home as I had ever traveled. I arranged to stay over after the five-day training to enjoy the island on the first solo vacation I had ever taken in all the years of my marriage. My wife, a teacher, could not get released from classes, and besides, she reasoned, we could not take the kids from their schoolwork for that long.

The story after this is both long and short. In my wanderings about the small island, often on nearly deserted, calendar-picture beaches, the Maker put in my path a young Hawaiian surfer, K. To the more jaded, which I had not yet become, the encounter was nothing more than a pickup by a young gay man cruising the beach and being attracted mysteriously to an older man with a beard and a winter-white, Appalachian body. Only later would I become aware that I was what some in the gay community would call a bear.

This young bear-lover had no idea what impact his presence that day, and for the next several days, would have in my life; and neither did I. My surfer boy, in his early twenties, released a part of me that even I did not know existed. To him,

I was just a pick-up on the beach. He could not have known where his actions would lead me.

Then, to borrow the words Annie Proulx writes of the reunion between Ennis and Jack after four years, " . . . easily as the right key turns the lock tumblers," we kissed and caressed under the ironwoods that lined the surf-pounded beaches and sheltered us from the blazing sun sitting low in an azure sky punctuated that afternoon by scattered banks of cotton-puff clouds. He was the first man I had kissed in twenty-four years! It was the first sex I'd had with a man in even more years. Yet it seemed I had come home to myself. It was natural, instinctive, and right.

It somehow must have been more to him than even he first intended, or maybe he was only responding to my need. It really doesn't matter now. We spent the next several days together making love, holding hands, talking, and lying next to each other on rock-strewn cliffs overlooking blue, Pacific waters—me smelling the warmth of his sun-darkened skin and the sweet mix of suntan oils and musky sweat. My past came flooding back, and, without any real awareness of how my life was going to be in a week or a month, I knew a door had opened. I had walked—nay, run—through it and would not return. For those few days, I was like Ennis, "pawing the white out of the moon" and reveling in it despite knowing it would soon end. I never saw K again after those few days in paradise, but I had a new life that he and the Maker had given me. I had no idea what would happen next.

The encounter set many things in motion. It seems odd to admit it now, but till that moment when K's hand touched mine and we kissed in the shade of the ironwoods, I had not realized I had never actually fallen in love, or at least had not allowed myself to experience it consciously at full-throttle. I never realized that, despite my clinical empathy, I really did not know what people were talking about when that phrase was used. It took forty-seven years to make that discovery.

Brokeback Mountain brought many tears to my eyes. The recognition and regret that Ennis seems to have at the end reminded me of the wasted years of my life and how my own Alma was left to grow old alone. Moreover, I am reminded of the thousands of others whose lives were altered, were less fulfilling, and were loveless or lost because of how our culture treats homosexuality.

Now, when I hear a man say he won't go to see *Brokeback* because he doesn't want to see two men kissing, I wonder why it is that seeing two men kill each other in bloody combat is so much more acceptable. A gay combat-decorated Vietnam Vet, who died in 1988 and was finally buried with full honors in the Congressional Cemetery, has on his tombstone an inscription which he wrote himself: "When I was in the military, they gave me a medal for killing two men, and a discharge for loving one." Our world is strange beyond words, is it not?

I thank the Maker for putting K in my path, even if for a short time. I thank the Maker for J, whose rattled snores reassure me of his presence in our bed each night. I can reach out and touch the man I never dared to dream about. He is real! I only wish that Ennis had been so fortunate.

Dave (63) is a retired psychologist who lives with his partner of ten years, their two cats and two dogs, in West Virginia. Ironwood *is his screen name.*

23 Moving On and Opening Up

—atruant

Am I an Ennis or a Jack? I am neither, but possess elements of both.

To set the scene, let me say at the outset that I am a gay man who has never been able to form an emotional relationship or have sex with a woman, though not for lack of trying. Until recently, I have been firmly closeted. I am a Canadian, belonging to a society which is less homophobic than the United States.

I knew I was queer since before puberty, but it wasn't until high school that I really understood it. By that time, I had been in love with five boys. (I have a list of about twenty-five men I have seriously loved in my lifetime.) Early on, I developed the stare that Jack does so well when he was being the "stud duck" by the truck, casing Ennis at the beginning of the movie. At age sixteen, I had an Ennis-like reaction after a summer camp where a new friend and I had fallen in love (no sex). From that, I learned to temper my feelings with subsequent boyfriends. I was a tall, good-looking, and intelligent young man. I was a social guy and loved to dance, so having permanent, good-looking girlfriends was not an issue. I would fantasize I was with my current male friend, and maneuver my dancing partner near the guy so I could watch him. The scene when Jack first dances with Lureen and is shown with a faraway look really grabbed me, and I thought, "He's thinking of Ennis! Been there!" I went to high school in a large urban center where homosexuality was rarely a subject of conversation, and when it was, there was little derision.

I loved to fly and earned my private pilot's license in the mid-sixties at age eighteen. It was my dream to become a fighter pilot, and, of course, that meant joining the military. It was clear queers were not allowed, effectively closing the door on any thoughts of coming out back then. I was successful at university and at flying; I became a good fighter pilot, attending our own top gun school. For most of that time, I was paranoid, like Ennis, often wondering: the people in the street, do they know?

Early on in my flying career I met "Jim." At the time, I was sharing a house with two other military guys, one of whom I thought was gay. Of course we never talked about it, and I was not attracted to him. I'll call him "Greg." One night after a party, Greg got Jim into his bed overnight, and I thought, "Okay, Greg is gay." I later found out nothing happened. Greg will reappear twenty years later in my story.

Jim was an aircraft technician and drop-dead gorgeous. We became good friends and fell in love with each other over time. One night we partied and drank too much and ended up wrestling in bed. One thing led to another, and our seventeen-year relationship got off to a bouncing start. Jim is twice divorced, thrice married, no kids. Although we often lived on separate bases, our travels would mean that we could meet regularly. Both he and I realized that a "cow and calf operation" was not in the stars, and we were (and are) comfortable with that. I have loved other men, all straight, over the years, which does not affect what Jim and I will always share.

In the early nineties, the military ceased to oust people for being gay or lesbian. I was part of the policy formulation and had to work hard to contain my enthusiasm for it! By that time, I could discuss homosexuality without a pounding heart and hot face. Imagine my surprise when I saw a file about Greg cross my desk. Several months before the rule change, the military police had investigated him and found out he was openly gay. He was outed and ousted despite a spotless professional record. I sent him a note about the new policies, but he'd had enough and moved to western Canada, where he still resides. Bad timing for Greg, but I have to give the Canadian military top marks for forward thinking on this issue. In 2006, the first military gay marriages took place; and in the nineties, I started slowly to come out to the odd friend, although not to any professional colleagues. New policies can be legislated, but not old attitudes.

I've enjoyed emotional, loving relationships with men, which have resulted in a basically happy, stable life for me over the years. After my last flying tour in the late nineties, I was again posted to a desk job. A man, I'll call him "Chris," came to work for me. He was an outstanding performer, a good-looking athlete and body-builder. I am a runner, so we would often meet in the gym during the noon hour. He wanted a cardio workout, so he started running with me. His young kid and my dog were the same age, so with that as an excuse, I invited them over one weekend. Our friendship blossomed. I became friends with his wife, too, which is mostly the case with other close friends of mine. Chris really took to me—I could tell with the body language, the sweet smile, the shining eyes, and the gripping handshakes every time we met. I fell in love with him. He, our "kids," and I went camping one long weekend while his wife was studying for an exam. Over a roaring fire and a few beers, as we were solving all the world's problems, I told him I loved him as a friend, not indicating anything about being gay. He reciprocated. Sex would have rounded it off for me, but I was satisfied with our deep, loving friendship.

That said, I must admit to a lingering desire for a full relationship. A couple of years ago, I started to break out more by signing up with a few gay dating sites. I have made a couple of new friends by this means. I have rejected several offers. I have a standing offer from one man I respect to visit him any time, but he's made it clear he wants in my pants right off the bat. No thanks. Most guys seem to be looking for instant sex, but it's not the way I want to start.

Then *Brokeback Mountain* came along. Like so many other people, I identified with much of the story through its fictional characters. *Brokeback* made me experience the love and excitement that I can only feel for a man. It was a positive response that has empowered me to move on and to continue to open up my life.

On September 2, 2006, atruant updated his story:

As some of you know, over the last few months I have mentioned in posts that a fellow Forum member and I were engaging in a cyber-relationship, after having first made contact on the "Are You Jack or Ennis?" thread. We discovered we had much in common: single, 100% gay, never married, two pets each, celibate for many years, books, music, genealogy, and spirituality—dozens of psychic moments right from the start, and many others. It was, without doubt, our reaction to *Brokeback Mountain* and the lessons learned from it, as well as this Forum, that prompted us to meet despite living in different countries and on separate coasts. Furthermore, we were going to make it in August and not wait till November!

I live on Vancouver Island; he lives in Virginia Beach. Since it's pretty hot and humid there at this time of year, it made sense for him to visit me first. So I picked him up in Vancouver; we did some sightseeing there, ferried across to Victoria, did more touristy stuff, and then came to my place here in the Comox Valley.

We were both confident that the solid base of our friendship would manifest itself in the same way after meeting physically for the first time, and we were right. Webcam is great, but it doesn't compare to being face to face! It didn't take long before we "deepened our intimacy considerably" and found love. Since we had both been there before, we knew it was real. Both of us had wondered if love would ever happen again in our lives. Neither of us expected it to happen this way. Here is another example of "love finds you," rather than the other way around. Also, it's never too late. And there is enough time.

He and I are taking a step-by-step, phased approach to the future. There are numerous obstacles to overcome, not the least of which is distance. We miss each other so much we can hardly stand it, but we are going to fix it.

Atruant, 59, is retired and a former Canadian Air Force pilot who resides in British Columbia, Canada.

...never enough time, never enough.

24 Teach Your Children Well

Whether instructing in the classroom or teaching their own children, many Forum members share the lessons of Brokeback Mountain, *determined to reinforce in young and open minds the need for empathy and acceptance.*

Challenge, Teach, Celebrate

—therese

I have been thinking about the main thing I've learned from the movie and Forum, and that is to practice tolerance. I am pledging the following for my daily life as a result of seeing *Brokeback Mountain*:

1. If someone makes a prejudiced remark—be it racist, homophobic, sexist, anti-Semitic, anti-Muslim, or whatever—I will speak up and challenge them. I don't have to be aggressive about it, but I will let them know clearly that I and many others feel differently. It is too easy to hide behind silence.

2. I will teach my children tolerance, and from as young an age as they can understand it. I'll emphasize that love comes in many forms, and no one should be judged by whom and how they love.

3. I will use my work to celebrate difference and encourage its acceptance.

Train Eyes and Heart

—Poohbunn

I don't want to be known as a white woman. When someone sees me, I want them to think more than "aging hippy." I'm both, but much, much more. And more than that, I believe this is true of everyone.

I have been reading about how those who control the language control far more. Categories, pigeonholes—gay, bi, straight—are social constructs. They can be part of one's identity if one wants, but they aren't the person. It's wonderful when we train our eyes and heart to see the entire person instead of one feature.

It's too bad we can't teach that to kids in school. It would go a long way towards eliminating bigotry.

On Fire

—amymm

So along comes Pooh to help me segue into my next tangent. I also feel our children are inheriting more than a diseased planet, a bad war, and a huge debt. They are also inheriting an attitude that excludes people based on their categories. Since when is it okay to tell someone they aren't entitled to basic rights such as marriage? America should not be a place where rights are taken away.

My nine-year-old son wanted to know what *Brokeback Mountain* was about. I told him it was about two people in love who were told their love was wrong. He said "Oh, like *Holes*." *Holes* is a book and movie about a white woman and black man who fall in love in the 1800s. After their love is discovered, the man is killed, much like Jack in *Brokeback Mountain*. I told him it was similar, but *Brokeback Mountain* was about two men. He was surprised. He said, "I never heard of that before." I told him many people who are the same sex and in love don't feel comfortable expressing their love in the open, so he wouldn't see a lot of examples.

So the next day he said, "Mom, I've decided that I'm going to teach my children it's okay to love anyone you want." I told him that that's probably the most important thing you can teach your children. He smiled and then asked if he could have a doughnut at the store. Kids are pretty amazing. They really don't have any opinions other than ours. We do have the chance to reshape the world through them.

I'm on fire, and I'm not backing down.

Amy is a 36-year-old stay-at-home mom who is homeschooling her three children. She lives in the San Francisco Bay Area. She posts using the name amymm.

Finland's Next Generation

—Jari Koskisuu

The minimum age to see *Brokeback Mountain* in Finland is eleven. My friend's oldest daughter is fourteen. Her class sees two movies each semester together as part of the school curriculum. The students get to choose the movie—with teachers vetoing if necessary, of course. This time her whole class wanted to see *Brokeback Mountain*. The teachers resisted at first, but the class was adamant, and they all went to see it.

They thought that "the ending was stupid" because "why couldn't they be together?" They had good discussions, not about homosexuality, but about losing a friend, about what it means to fall in love, about harassment and violence, and about what it is like to be perceived as different. My friend is divorced, and she said that for the first time her daughter had shared her feelings about it with her classmates and later with her.

But why had the teachers objected at first? They were afraid of the reaction of parents. There was no parental written consent procedure beforehand. Not one parent had complained, not one.

Thank God for the next generation. Sometimes I am proud of living here up north.

Forty-four-year-old Jari Koskisuu, who lives with his partner in Helsinki, Finland, works in the rehabilitation field. He posts using the screen name Boris.

Canadian Lesson Plan

—sinne

Brokeback Mountain is being used as a teaching tool in high schools. Hurray! Makes me proud to be a Canadian—again!

The British Columbia Teachers' Federation (BCTF) Homophobia and Heterosexism Action Group has developed a *Brokeback Mountain* Lesson Plan, the first time BCTF has built a lesson plan around a movie. It points out that children need to be fourteen or over in Canada to view the film. The lesson plan is aimed for grades ten to twelve.

Stated learning outcomes of the lesson plan are to encourage students: (1) to analyze how this movie reflects current-day attitudes towards gay people, (2) to understand how homophobia impacts people's daily lives, and (3) to encourage student's personal choices in making the world more accepting of GLBT people.

Among the questions given for discussion among students after viewing the film are the following: What factors influence homophobia in rural communities? How would they be similar to your school community? To what degree has life changed for GLBT rural youth since 1963 when this movie was set? What needs to change in society before Jack Twist's dream of him and Ennis owning a ranch together would be a non-event in a rural community?

Sinne, 52, lives in British Columbia, Canada and loves film.

Bonds of Friendship

—brokebackLJ

I was with a few friends after rehearsal last night, and there is this guy I've been friends with since last semester—just an acquaintance, but a really nice guy. We've been talking a lot more since rehearsals have started, as he is one of the leads in the show. So he, I, and two girls decided to hang out last night and drink a few beers.

We began talking about *Brokeback Mountain*, and this guy said, "You know, LJ, when I saw you the other day with your cowboy hat, I envied you. I thought you looked really good. I think I should get one!" Up until then, most of my friends have been making fun of my *Brokeback Mountain* obsession. We then proceeded to have this huge conversation about being gay, straight, bi, in this world and how awesome it is to have *Brokeback Mountain* in my life. He said, "You know, I was in the gay/straight alliance in my high school. I'm comfortable with being straight, but people always seem to think I'm gay, by the way, you know, I take care of how I look." He said he feels that people usually think of him as a metrosexual, and it bothers him a lot. As a straight man, it pisses him off that there are so many gender roles and pressures for people to live up to in our society. There is always this pressure that society imposes on us to be more masculine.

When we "got to drinking and talking," I had an experience I don't recall ever having before: non-sexual bonding with a straight man. I'm not used to thinking of men in strictly platonic terms. I've grown up with a fear of straight men and have had a hard time trying to relate to them or trying to be close with them, because I always fear that they think I'm coming on to them or that I'm wanting more out of the relationship, and it makes them uncomfortable. This friend of mine says that for him it doesn't matter— gay/straight/bi, whatever—there is a human need for men to have bonds with other men, just as women do with other women. I don't think I've really felt that before until last night. It might sound like I'm romanticizing him, but I'm not. I'm touched and excited that another guy, who doesn't have a sexual interest in me, wants to be my friend because he enjoys my company. It's really refreshing: with most of the guys I meet, there is a sexual attraction, and they want something based on that. So it's hard to have guy friends.

Most of my best friends are girls, because there isn't any sexual tension. I don't sense any tension between me and this guy. I've never had a crush on him. He's always been this really great guy, whom I enjoy more and more every time I talk to him. I'm happy to have found a connection, as he calls it, that doesn't have anything to do with sexuality. It's just two people, and people will always find ways of relating and coming together. Why can't two people just connect without it having to be defined as gay or straight?

Teach Your Children Well   155

Proud Mom

—Meira

I took my fourteen-year-old daughter to see *Brokeback Mountain*. Both my kids and husband are amused and puzzled by the amount of time I spend on this board, playing the soundtrack over and over, and downloading pictures of Jake and Heath. She's in her last year of middle school—thank God!—and the "that's so gay" phrase they all like to throw around is something I've been lecturing against to no avail. She's a sensitive kid, though, and I thought she could handle the movie, so we went.

Halfway through, she was sniffling. When the postcard came back marked "deceased," she started sobbing and didn't stop till we left the theater. She talked all the way home about how she feels sorry for Ennis and Jack. "How can Ennis bear to live?" She declared that she thinks he'll commit suicide. "How can he live without Jack?" I pointed out to her that she was talking about them as if they were real people, not movie characters, to give her a mirror, and she paused to say, "But they were so real; it didn't feel like a movie." It was a lot for her to think about, but the next day when she heard her brother (who is almost eleven) use that phrase, she jumped all over him! It meant a lot more than Mom coming down on him, I can tell you! I'm really proud of her.

Meira, 48, is a volunteer special education advocate who lives with her husband and two children in Eastern Massachusetts.

25 That Old Boat

—Osprey

We would both turn eighteen that summer, in August. We were both masculine, lettermen in athletics. Michael was 6 feet, 1 inch, slim, with brown curly hair and deep blue eyes. I was 5 feet 10 inches, slim, white blond hair, green eyes and the olive skin of my Swiss German heritage. He was rugged and hyper-masculine and was as darkly beautiful as Ennis is light. There were times when the sun hit his face from a certain angle, or his hair, and it would make me catch my breath. When we were growing up in a small town of 8,000 people on the border of Utah, Colorado, and Wyoming, our families did everything together.

There was no evolution to our physical relationship. We went from zero to off the scale in one night. We drank that first little bottle of vodka in our sodas that night. Neither of us had ever touched another human being in a sexual way before. But when, side by side, we faced the sun that next morning, we were lovers in every way known to man, and nothing would ever be the same again. Pandora had opened the box, and the hope and troubles were already spread halfway across Wyoming.

The first night Michael and I made love, we were on my family's ski boat. It had a huge rear deck and we often slept out there when we went fishing. I lost track of the boat while I was away at college. Michael and I were lovers for twelve years.

By the time I was twenty-three I knew I was gay. There was no question about it, and I wanted to come out to my family. Like everyone else who has gone through coming out, I was afraid: afraid of losing my family, my friends, just about everything I cherished. My father was an amazing man, the best thing and the worst thing that happened to all of us. He was a rebel, he was a tyrant, he was a genius; he never finished the eighth grade, yet he had his first million dollars by the time he was thirty. He was hard to live with. He was the ultimate macho self-made businessman rancher.

The few close friends that I had come out to were terrified for me. They felt my father would disown me, beat me to death, cast me to the wolves, never speak to me again. They felt that my mother would be powerless to stop him. I feared they might well be right, but I had enough of dad running through my own veins that I figured the earlier I knew where I stood, the better off I would be. If I was going to be totally on my own, it would be better to know it at twenty-three than, say, forty-five, when I might be involved in a family business, married or God knows what, and be cast into outer darkness with half my life gone. The thought of playing "Let's pretend I'm straight" did not appeal to me. No one at that time had any reason to think I was gay, but I didn't want to live with the daily fear of being found out.

I called dad and told him I needed to talk to him in private. He said that he had to go to an outlying ranch that afternoon, and I could go along. He picked me up, and for the first few miles we made small talk. Finally, I just came out and said it: "Dad, I'm gay." There was an ominous silence for about a quarter of a mile and then he said, "So? You've always been a happy kid." Shit. I couldn't believe it. I had finally had the guts to say the words and it was a dry run. "No, dad, that isn't the kind of gay I am talking about."

He adjusted his hat. You always knew the fur was about to fly when he started to mess with his hat. "Dad, I'm a homosexual."

He looked straight ahead and put both hands back on the steering wheel. I was amazingly tranquil; I sat there watching him and waiting for the blows to start falling. After a few seconds, he just turned and looked at me. "You mean you like to have sex with men?" "Yes" was all I could bring myself to say. We drove on for what seemed like forever before he finally spoke. "You know, son, dogs and pigs screw; it isn't much of a claim to fame. Now if I ever hear of you stealing, lying to hurt someone, being cruel to your family, or failing to do something productive with your life, or failing to leave the world a better place, then we will have a problem. But, son, while I think your life would be easier if you liked women, I don't care if you screw sheep as long as you don't do it on Main Street."

I could hardly wrap my mind around what I was hearing. He went on to impart to me wisdom I have carried to this day. "Son, the religions get all riled up and focus on things we have in common with animals, and that is why I never pay them much mind. I am more interested in the things we have in common with God, like the ability to be fair, to be honest, to be kind, to work hard for things that leave the world a better place. Our appetites are things we have in common with all animals and, while they should be filled responsibly, whether it's screwing or food, at the end of the day they don't mean diddly to who you are as a man."

Although I came out to my family, not one single human being knew about Michael and me. It could have gone on forever, I guess, but I reached a point where I couldn't handle it any more. I wanted a life, and I didn't want a life based on a lie. I ended the relationship eighteen years ago. I left our hometown for several years, as I knew I wouldn't have the strength to stay away from him.

When I moved back home, he was married. We had a long talk and committed to remaining friends. He was married for only five years.

We saw each other often. When I met my wonderful companion, Marty, Michael welcomed him into my life. Michael never seemed envious of my relationship, but I knew that he suffered horribly, and I felt frustrated, as I never could figure out a way to change things. I have never known anyone who could suffer so deeply in such utter silence.

He was fragmented and haunted because he could never deal with the fact that he was gay. Living in our rural Western town didn't help much. He jumped from one dead-end job to another. Michael was not a leader, yet he could not be led. The more books you bought him the more pages he ate. He never got it together in his entire life.

Michael killed himself on the fifth of July, 2004. Two weeks before he took his life, this terrible feeling came over me. I tracked him down and asked him to come by my office to talk. He sat there and lied through his teeth. I knew in my heart he was lying, but I was helpless against his stoicism. His life had turned into a confusing, desperate lie and finally, at forty-four, he put a high-powered rifle under his chin and ended it.

Michael is the private hell I have carried around inside me for most of my life. It is a place that I have never let anyone go with me until now. The primary reason was to protect Michael. As long as he was alive, I felt an obligation not to force his hand, not to force him out of the closet. He had a wife, though they had divorced, and a daughter. Who was I to expose him to them or anyone else?

Michael's love for his beautiful daughter was not enough to keep him going. She was the center of his universe, and he worshiped her. But once he decided that things beyond her existence made it impossible to go on, it was as if she no longer existed. He turned and walked out of our lives, her life, without even a goodbye, no note, nothing—as if we never mattered at all. I have this terrible feeling that once a certain point is reached, once a certain boundary is crossed, that is just the way it is. I hope to God I am wrong.

His funeral was the hardest thing I have ever done in my life. It was horrible knowing that I was the only person there who understood what had happened and why. He left no note, and to this day his daughter and ex-wife have no clue as to who he really was.

After Michael died, the family was going through his few possessions. He had an old farm equipment shed at Brush Creek. Under a dirty tarp, at the very back of that rickety shed, they found that old boat. When they called and asked if I knew its significance, I could hardly speak. In all those years, he had never once told me he loved me, but I guess that old boat pretty much said it.

We lost dad three years ago. He loved my companion Marty like a son. They were thicker than thieves. They would take off and be gone all day together and come home stinky, dirty as pigs, and happy as clams.

Now I am in a rich, rewarding relationship. My companion of fourteen years and I live openly in that same small town in Utah. Twenty years ago, it would have been unthinkable that we could live openly as a gay couple here, but we have never had a second's problem.

Rance, 46, and his partner, Marty, live in northeastern Utah, where they run a very successful business focused on ornamental flora needs.

It's because of you, Jack, that I'm like this.

26 Inspired to Change

In the weeks and months after their first experience of Brokeback Mountain, *what Ennis and Jack had, and what they could never have, inspired viewers worldwide to examine their own dissatisfactions, traumatic memories, and ongoing fears. Many for the first time found the power to confront and overcome them.*

Before and Since

—Jay63

I now view life as *before* and *since Brokeback.*

Life Before—if one could call it life:

At forty-two, I've known for almost thirty years that I am gay, but was never able to accept it. I isolated myself completely from intimate relationships, especially from gay men. I lived in mortal fear of being outed and alienated from my large and homophobic rural family. It never worried me much that my small and progressive circle of friends and colleagues would care one way or the other what my sexuality was, though I still avoided the subject. It was simply my own homophobic mindset keeping me imprisoned.

During my late thirties, out of desperation for companionship, I dated an amazing woman, but cut that off when she hinted at wanting more than a platonic friendship. It has been nothing but lonely slices of pie in too many sad cafés for me since then. That scene with Cassie confronting an elusive Ennis struck home. Never wanting to lead a double life, I have "put the blocks" to no one, man or woman. Of course, it is clear now that a double life is exactly what I've been living all these years. Oh my God, what a waste of valuable time—and for what? I spent the last two decades diverting my energies into work, wrapping my whole identity in it, and ultimately that was no longer enough to sustain me. Late last year, I was trying my best to be happy, but in reality I was "nothin, nowhere." All this time, I was also neglecting my health, killing myself slowly with regular thoughts of speeding up the end.

In mid-February, for the fifth viewing, I tagged along with a couple of female friends. Not wanting to see it alone again, I had outed myself for the first time. At long last, I had turned a corner. Realizing that I was like Ennis in that dank trailer, starkly alone, I knew I needed to decide if I would continue to choose the self-destructive path or learn from the lesson Jack and Ennis—and Annie Proulx—were offering.

Since then:

- I have lost seventy-five pounds, with seventy-five pounds yet to go.
- I have hired a health/life coach to guide me as I rebuild my life.
- I bought a bicycle and ride it daily.
- I have renewed energy in my work, but am trying to strike a balance with other activities.
- I began to volunteer some time to a non-profit organization, and here's the best news—I met a great guy and asked him if he'd like to see a movie or go to a concert sometime. He said yes! We had our first date a couple weeks later. It seems we have lots in common, and being out with him seems so natural.
- I have come out to a number of friends. All have been powerfully affirming. I'm not out to any family yet—still debating how to tackle that.

None of this would have happened if not for *Brokeback Mountain*.

Jay is a 42-year-old artist from Cleveland, Ohio, who has traveled and exhibited widely throughout the USA.

Opened Doors

—OnesEnough

The movie opens doors through which oceans of experience gush in, doors that millions of people have had difficulty in slamming shut and holding closed with their backs against it. Imagine a horror movie: she's in the bathroom trying to keep the door shut against the pounding demons and horror behind the door. *Brokeback Mountain* makes you step away from the door and realize the demons can only hurt you if you are afraid of them.

This author is a 45-year-old man from Istanbul, Turkey.

Choices Define Us

—brokebackLJ

I'm nineteen. I came out when I was fourteen. We go through a lot that shapes who we are, how we view gay people, and how we relate to others and have relationships. Growing up in a small town, where I came out, I've had so much emotional and personal shit to deal with. I was met with a lot of tension and hate. It scared me. To this day I have a hard time accepting and loving myself.

While *Brokeback Mountain* shows me what not to do, it also shows me that there isn't just one type of gay man: that there is connection to be found and shared between two people that no one else can verbalize, not even the people involved. *Brokeback Mountain* showed me that there are people out there who will love you for who you are, despite all your flaws and tragedies. And that life and relationships aren't easy. There isn't always one happy ending. But the choices we make define us, and sometimes we have choices for a happier future.

Took Away My Fear

—Luis A. Rodriquez

Today I came out to my sister. The reason is *Brokeback* and this Forum. It made me think: "What the heck! Why shouldn't I be open with the people I love? Why should I be ashamed of anything?" And that took away my fear.

She wasn't the least surprised. She confessed that the idea of me being gay had popped into her mind lately, but that she would have dismissed it if I hadn't told her the truth.

She split up with her husband six years ago, and I think she still loves him. She has been suspicious for the longest time that her ex-husband could also be gay, like Ennis, not knowing how to speak to himself and avoiding acceptance of the truth. She told me this with a flood of tears in her eyes, telling me how sorry she felt for Alma when she sees Ennis and Jack kissing each other. How terrible it is to live carrying our lies on our backs, and how refreshing and wonderful it is to be truthful.

Brokeback has made me a better person, happier and more trusting.

Luis A. Rodríguez, 47, is a Catholic Brother and linguist from Basque Country in the European Union. He posts under the screen name Basqueboy.

Coming Out as a Human Being

—Darryl Dravland

Yesterday I called my sis, who is the oldest in the family now that our parents are gone, and talked to her about our family and *Brokeback*. We both had a difficult time when our mother passed some eight years ago, and we found solace and comfort in our private conversations that helped pull us through. But we have only discussed my personal life once before. Last night, we talked for two hours!

I talked about *Brokeback Mountain,* and how much it was helping me get through horrible memories that have come back to me from growing up.

Before *Brokeback*, I wasn't able to bring all this stuff up. I would have held it in. But now I am opening up to friends and family as I have never before. Those hauntings from yesteryear are being dealt with now. Isn't it amazing?

Do I want to miss opportunities any more? No!

Do I want to hold back from saying how I feel about something, as long as it's appropriate? No!

Do I want to be a complete human and also be treated like one? Hell, yes!

This all feels like another coming out, not out of the closet as gay, but as a human being. I'm not feeling second-rate any more.

Darryl Dravland, 54, is a single man living in Cincinnati. He is passionate about helping those afflicted with alcohol and drug-related problems.

A Brighter Path

—Chris Lattanzio

For much of my life, I have meditated both at home and out in my native forests here in Staten Island. Recently, I feel I am on the brink of understanding something, grasping a thread of what life is made of.

We think we have to live up to things or for other people, so they will be proud or happy. But what about us? What about our pains and sorrows and loves and lives? All we can do in this life is to live it for ourselves. I have been searching for a path both to life and to enlightenment; after seeing *Brokeback*, I feel as if that path has been made a little brighter. I realized that my affinity with nature was something I really love and not just as a hobby. So part of this path has been to embrace that need to be surrounded by raw life. How I am going to get to that point I am still not sure.

I have come out to my family, but it has been more of a "don't ask, don't tell" sort of coming out. Before *Brokeback*, I never brought who I was into the home. Imagine a 23-year-old afraid to read a book or watch a TV channel because of what people might think.

The biggest thing *Brokeback* has given me is my freedom. I have bought gay movies and books and even subscribed to *The Advocate*. Gay isn't who I am, but it is a part of me, a part I want to be able to keep even in my family home. And now I do.

The world will change in its own time. All I can change right now is myself. To feel bad about something, to regret the past, or to fear the future is useless. That is what I get from watching *Brokeback*: a shake from a drowsy embrace.

Chris Lattanzio is a 24-year-old graphic artist from New York who is responsible for this book's artwork. He is currently working his way through graduate school. He is an avid photographer. He posts under the screen name ChrisFewa.

My Loving Sister

—couzins43

I'm in the process of coming out after many years of denial. My sister is going through a rough time as well. She's going through a bad divorce. We hadn't spoken for about three weeks, but today she called, upset.

In the process of calming her down, I told her that I've wanted to call her but have been going through a rough patch myself. She started to pry, and insisted I at least give her a clue. I didn't know what clue to give her, so I said it: "I'm gay." I didn't want to tell her over the phone, but this is how it happened. Her response was ". . . and?" She said she's known or felt it for some time, but didn't want to be the one to bring it up. She felt I needed to do it in my own time. She said that my being gay would never make her stop loving me and that she was proud of me for coming out to her. She would be there for me no matter what. You can imagine my tears.

I know I will have the support of one of the most important members of my family: my beautiful, loving sister. I don't know what else to say other than I'm out now. I still have a long journey ahead, but I think it's going to be all right now. I guess the old saying "What doesn't kill you makes you stronger" may be true after all.

Seize the Day

—liketoday

This film has empowered gay men, made us realize how much more we could be doing to help people around us to seize the day and change their reality to become happy with who they are.

I don't think its message or lesson is relevant only to gay people in the closet. Because of this film, I've communicated some important truths to some people in my family who are straight but miserably unhappy. Two weeks ago, I knew they had this problem—heck, it's been dragging on for years—and had persisted in the attitude that it's their problem and I'm not getting involved. Now, because of how different I feel, I thought, f**k it, I'm going to say something!

I'm amazed by how positive their response to me has been. They're touched to find that someone cares enough to say anything!

This author is 34 years old and hails from Paris, France.

Finding True Love

—Diego

I'm twenty-one, and I'm still in the closet.

I'm pretty much one of the guys. I'm not remotely interested in the gay scene. I don't hate it. It's just not my thing. Even though I'm in L.A., for me it's pretty hard to find anyone like myself. So I've never had a boyfriend. Before I saw *Brokeback Mountain*, I felt I would end up alone. I never thought I would find a guy and have a fulfilling relationship. And now as I type this, I hate myself for giving up that dream without a fight.

When I read "Brokeback Mountain" and saw the film, I was side-punched. I never thought that a gay relationship could be portrayed like that: that real, that touching. I remember thinking about how beautiful their love was. It gave me a taste of what I desperately wanted. Something clicked. And that night for the first time in my life I finally started to think about who I was and what I wanted in life. The idea of finding true love came back to my mind, that it was a possibility for me. I don't think I would have realized this if not for *Brokeback*.

The younger generation has a lot to gain from this movie. There are a lot of us, like me, who have never dealt with being gay and have given up on ever finding true love. This film can help my peers realize how horrible that state of mind can be.

I guess you could say that *Brokeback Mountain* helped me come out of the closet to myself.

Diego is a 21-year-old man from California.

Reclaim Our Direction

—Boris

*B*rokeback provided us with a language of loss that we all could understand. *Brokeback* hit us directly in the heart and ripped our protective layers to shreds. It left us vulnerable and raw, but also alive. *Brokeback* cannot give meaning or purpose to our lives, but it has exposed the need, shown us that we may have lost our direction and we need to reclaim it.

Forty-four-year-old Jari Koskisuu, who lives with his partner in Helsinki, Finland, works in the rehabilitation field. He posts under the screen name Boris.

Responding to one married Forum member who was trying to reach a decision about coming out, another member gave encouragement in the form of his own coming-out story.

Discovering Yourself

—Tulienm

*S*omething in one of your recent posts sort of hit me and made me feel like I might be able to help—or not. I'm sixty now. I've had my Ennis all roped and hogtied for many, many years. I might just get ambitious one day and write a whole page or two about how wonderful he is, but that's not what this is about. You said: "I need to figure this thing out for myself." Thus begins the adventure. You, on your own, must chart a course through one of the last frontiers, the land of men who love men.

In retrospect, being a guy who loves another guy has been the best thing that ever happened to me. It forced me beyond what I might have otherwise been. We are given a blueprint at birth, and allowing for some modifications and variations, most people stay pretty much on course. My brother and sister did. I took one look at the blueprint and said "No can do." Not for me. From that moment on I had to deconstruct the world as I knew it and put it together again in a way that made sense for me. I was forced to question the world around me and my place in it. I came to the conclusion that there was room for improvement in the world, and in me, but we were both basically beautiful. And so are you.

It would have been easy for me to marry Marsha, my high school sweetheart, have 2.5 children, drive the Wonder Bread truck in Moses Lake, Washington, until I retired, then die of heart failure on my way to Yellowstone in the RV. It would have been a life, and maybe a good one. Instead, I—and you also—chose a much more difficult path. We have to make up the rules as we go along. I actually find it exciting. We have to utilize all our mental and physical resources to make the best decisions. We have to stretch. You are going to be amazed at the strength of character you are going to discover in yourself. It's there.

Whatever happens, you are already blessed by having kids. My guy was married for ten years and has a son and daughter. We even have grandkids. They are a huge part of our life. I meddle in their business at every opportunity. We have never felt the need to explain or apologize for being together. We haven't done anything wrong. The kids have lived with us from time to time, and live close enough to get in on our weekly barbecues, and they have seen the calm, peaceful, intensely loving relationship their Dad and I have.

I could only wish the same for them and for you. I would like to finish by quoting a Father's Day card my grandson made for me: "My grampa is tall as a rocket blasting off into space. My grampa is as fun as going to Chucky Cheese and playing air hockey. My grampa is as strong as ten bulls charging at a rocket. My grampa is as funny as a professional clown." I treasure the words and the kid more than I could ever say. Your day is coming, and I think the right man will be by your side to share it. Good luck.

27 Bobby's Journey

—Bobby19in1963

I was nineteen in 1963, gay, and afraid to admit it. As a naïve, closeted gay man in those days, I did a lot of drinking to release those inhibitions and try to find some relief. Then in the sixties, still totally messed up with my sexuality, I got married.

That was so, so long ago—a lifetime ago. Now I'm older, and I find myself having been married for decades to a wonderful woman in a marriage that has satisfied neither of us. Then this wonderful movie comes along and wastes me! This movie made me face up to the fact that I've lied to myself all my life and have never found, for even a minute, the wonderful happiness Ennis and Jack have when they are first together. I had repressed those thoughts for so long that when I saw them on the screen my heart almost broke.

I hadn't cried in so long that I had forgotten how warm tears are. My pain was for me and for my wife, that we had not been able to have what Ennis and Jack had: that deep, abiding love, their hearts knit together so tightly. And I knew that it was my fault, just as it was Ennis's fault that he and Jack could never be together permanently.

It is strange that this movie could make me feel gay, but on the other hand could make me want so much for my wife and me to have that deep love that we both deserve. In fact, it made me feel that perhaps there was a way to transcend all of this and call it person-to-person love: the kind I know I can have.

The movie is literally changing my life, and there are so many thoughts going on that it is hard to compose them. Feeling this exquisite pain so deeply for the first time, and allowing it to wash over me, was cathartic. For the first time in my life, I have told a friend that I think I am gay: I came out to an old high school friend who came back into my life recently after forty-five years. She says nothing happens by accident. I made excuses to my wife and went with my friend in secret to see the movie. I had to see it on the big screen. We were both in tears at the end.

The pain that these men feel when they are apart is the pain I feel, but I don't have someone to completely lose myself in several times a year. I suppose that is why the movie is killing me with pain I have never, in all my life, allowed myself to feel.

Brokeback Mountain has done something to me with which I need help. I'm haunted by it. I feel as if I've missed something so sweet and precious in my life that it makes me sad, so sad I have trouble functioning sometimes.

Because of this movie and what it has done to my thinking, I am ready to consider seeing someone who can help me work it all out.

I'm finding that I want to improve myself: lose some weight, get physically fit, and begin anew on my book from a different perspective. I guess in the back of my mind I want to make myself more . . . I hate to say the word "attractive," but I guess that's it. I want to attract people to me because I'm a good human being, with a depth of love in my soul. This movie shook me out of my lethargy. I used to be so positive, but, as time went on, it didn't seem to be worth the effort. Now, all of a sudden, it is!

===

I wanted to bring everyone up to date on my journey. There have been ups and downs over the past two months, but today I am living on a positive note that rings true and clear to my heart and mind.

I can now say unequivocally that the feelings I've had for as long as I can remember have been those of a gay man. How hard was that to say? It must have been pretty hard, because I've been around six decades now.

Let's see, to whom have I come out? Old friends from high school whom I reconnected with at a recent homecoming reunion (they've been wonderfully supportive, way beyond what they might have been in our youth) and some gay men and women in my church. I've made friends at Parents, Families, and Friends of Lesbians and Gays (PFLAG).

I have not yet figured out how to come out to my family and other close friends, but I have been assured that there is no rush, since everyone has a different timeline, and mine is mine to figure out.

I'm exercising daily and feel so much better that it is hard to describe.

For those who are religious, I count Jesus as my best Friend and fellow traveler on this road leading to what I hope is somewhere much better. I got up in church last week and testified to these changes in me, without giving out any secrets, and how wonderful it was to have Jesus right beside me, saying that he loved me just the way I was. For now, that's good enough for both of us. I have lived in a strict religious community for the past thirty years; this wonderful change in my mind has freed me to think of all kinds of possibilities.

I have been unwilling to announce to the world on this Forum that I am a gay Mormon, caught in what I am calling my *"Brokeback Mountain* Mormon Marriage,"* but there, it's out.

This is the hardest thing I've had to face in my life.

Religion adds a dimension to the *Brokeback Mountain* phenomenon that makes it complicated for us believers. As soon as it is widely known by people I know that I am gay, there will be all kinds of repercussions.

All of the jobs in the church locally are done by people like me. I have held many positions in the church leadership and, because of that, I am widely known in my area. I have trained hundreds of pre-missionary youth for their missions and have a wide network of acquaintances because of that. For me to be openly gay is going to send ripples through this wide list of contacts that will shock them all. Persecution comes in all kinds of forms and in all kinds of places, and religious persecution totally sucks.

===

Am I happier? *You bet!* Am I living through a "g-d-damned bitch of an unsatisfactory situation?" *You bet!* Is there hope? *You bet!*

In the meantime, I have lots of options. I can continue as I am: hidden, closeted, miserable. I can come out to my wife, and we can keep it secret from everyone else and live with it. I can acknowledge fully who I am, and let the chips fall where they may, meaning that I would probably be asked to leave the church. And there are probably lots of areas in between. I don't know from day to day, and that's how I'm living right now.

I saw a wonderful therapist yesterday. Early in the conversation, he said, "My husband and I." If you remember, I only identified to myself that I was gay a couple of months ago, so I'm still quite the newbie on all of this. I felt my heart leap in my chest with some kind of happy emotion.

We were able to cut directly to the chase. He hypothesized about what it might be like to go home and tell my wife of forty years that I am unhappy and ask for a divorce. I would say that it didn't have to be soon; we could take a couple of years, if necessary, to get all the finances and insurance policies worked out, but that she could think about it while I went to do my exercise and could give me an answer when I returned.

Whoa! I've come a long way since my first viewing of *Brokeback Mountain*. On the way back to work from the therapist it all sank in, and I cried perhaps my first real, sad tears for me and my wife and family, knowing that to be happy we'll have to go in different directions from now on. That was a sobering dose of reality. I guess it goes from one baby step to another, and soon I'll be where I want to be.

===

I'm extremely thankful that I've encountered this movie at a time and place where I could dwell completely in its shadow and where I could open my heart and my mind to new concepts and thoughts. Having done this, I am now at a different place in life.

Life is not fair: we all know that. We just have to live it the best we can.

I think that's where I am now. I am getting my physical body in better shape—much better shape this year than last—so that if I get into a fight with somebody, perhaps I will feel better about winning. I've dropped sixty-five pounds. I got into a swimsuit for the first time in my eleven-year-old granddaughter's life and went swimming.

===

Admitting I was gay to myself and to others has taken me to a different world altogether, full of so many emotions that it's overwhelming at times. I'm approaching the forty-first anniversary of my "*Brokeback* Marriage" in a week. So where am I?

I am gathering information for my divorce attorney, so that we can figure out where I am and where I need to be. My life is going to change dramatically.

I vacillate, feeling so much sadness coming for so many family and friends, and it is hard to stay upbeat.

[*Bobby had a cancer scare, but his doctor told him that the tests were negative.*] If this all turns out to be a wonderful warning of my mortality, then I hope to use every minute from now on to improve my life.

===

I was unhappy with my life, and *Brokeback Mountain* promised salvation.

I remember a post on this Forum about how the ego can take a hit and leave you reeling, but that it quickly regains control of your thinking and drags you quickly back to the familiar haunts in your mind. It took about two weeks for me to begin to doubt and return, and over the months I rationalized and rationalized and then decided it was too painful. I'd head back into the closet.

After all, I told myself, life is good, family is great, friends are fine. We have a saying in my church: when all is not well we still say, "All is well in Zion, all is well . . . ."

===

I'm having an unusually hard time saying what I want to say tonight. *Brokeback Mountain* took me by storm. I wallowed in it and felt all of this new freedom and opportunity, and then I was jerked back to real life when I contemplated divorce and saw the attorney. That sobered me up from the obvious drunk I had been on with *Brokeback*. That seems a little harsh, but it was like some kind of drug, changing my thinking, giving me new feelings and new thoughts, and it was terribly addictive.

I've tried to go back in the closet, and it appears I'm damned if I do and damned if I don't. It is a lot harder than I realized at first, all of this thinking and decision-making that I never had to do as long as I was willing to be in the closet. When I'm in a manic mood, I think, what the hell—throw caution to the winds and *do it!* I revel in the mania, but I have to be careful not to do anything while there that will hurt me when I come down from the clouds back to reality.

So I guess I'm going to have to fess up and get with my psychologist and set out a plan to work it all out. I'm still holding at a sixty-five pound weight loss. It's tough, but with a little help from my friends, it is working. This is about the point when I've failed before and put all the weight back on and then some. I'm not going to do that this time, though.

I found a great psychologist, I had a couple of good friends who knew the new me, and I had all of my friends on this Forum, and I thought that that would be enough. It isn't enough. Once the genie was out of the bottle, once I had decided I am a gay man, there was no going back. And I firmly believe now that no matter how painful, in order to live with myself, I have to be myself—and that's a gay man.

I fooled myself into thinking that I could make do with the "*Brokeback* Marriage" that I have . . . but I just can't any longer. I need someone to love and someone to love *me*.

Bobby, an executive assistant from Phoenix, Arizona, is married, blessed with children and grandchildren and is a well-known community activist.

...if you want me to take his ashes up there on Brokeback ... I'd be proud to.

28 Life Is Not a Dress Rehearsal

As a result of watching Brokeback Mountain, *many viewers, both gay and straight, single or partnered, found they had a need to examine their lives and their relationships.*

Caring, Loving Men

—Jaybanks

Since seeing *Brokeback*, I find myself looking at men with uncontrollably dopey eyes. You couldn't get any dopier than my eyes right now. Young, old, and in-between, they're all fair game. Men are actually human. They're not just pieces of meat anymore. They are loving, adorable, and perfect in every way again. Does that fellow at the bus stop have a past love? Is that lawyer with the wedding band keeping any secrets? What locker room will that hottie be showering in tonight? Where did I go wrong? Where did I lose the ability to think that men are capable of loving?

Where have the egocentric pigs gone? Suddenly, I don't see men like that any more. *Brokeback* washed them clean away. All I see now are caring, loving men.

A Great Rush

—Beethovenrox1770

Life has opened up. I've dated for the first time in my life! I've lost over thirty pounds, and I've worked my ass off! I am in two plays, and I am recording my third CD. Such a great rush began and has continued since that cataclysmic night back in midJanuary.

Finally Moved My Arse

—Jack Schilling

For the first time in a long time, I feel hope. I had shut down completely without realizing it. Few things affected me, aside from my relatives; as for myself, I just existed. That's all—existed. This morning I woke up happy, really happy for the first time in a long time.

Here I am living in one of the world's most fascinating cities, and I was simply doing nothing and going nowhere. I've made arrangements to see some people who meant a great deal in my life. If nothing but re-established friendships come of this, I will be one happy SOB. If that turns out to be impossible, well, I can't fix it and will just have to stand it. The point is, I will have made an attempt, an adult attempt. And that's all a guy can do.

I made a decision to get in contact with the guy who had been my one and only. I felt that the worst that could happen was that nothing would come of it, and at least I would know. Did I want a sexual relationship? No, I can't say that I did. What I needed was the emotional closeness with this specific person. So I took the risk. Would he call back? I figured it might take a week, or that it might never happen. But he called back within 15 minutes.

We hadn't set eyes on each other for four years. This relationship was so important; I had never had another guy, never had sex with anyone else afterwards, never even wanted to. Was it obsessive? No. My feeling was that nothing else would ever come close to that love, and I wasn't going to settle for a glass of vinegar after wine. This was a once-in-a-lifetime sort of love.

The risk was worth it, the feeling was mutual; we met last Monday, and the bond came out full blown on both sides. We are both older and wiser.

Sex? No. He's married now. I can live with no sex between us, and so can he. We both have too much self-respect to destroy something else that is good when there is no need to do so. What we both needed and still need is to know that the love is there, that the love is real, that no matter what, our love is here to stay.

One week after seeing *Brokeback*, I had a sit-down with the woman I should have married years ago, untold years ago. We had been after each other since we were nineteen years old. That's thirty years. Through thick and thin, we had loved each other. The only bad patches were caused by "secrets": when we kept secrets, it did not go well. We had cared for each other all through her marriage to a genuine shithead, and all through the years when I was hammered every night. I had fallen in love with her and never allowed anything to grow out of fear. I was afraid I wouldn't measure up. Later, her bank account kept putting me off: I was too poor to damage my pride by being with someone so wealthy. I didn't want nameless people whispering that I'd married her for her trust fund.

At my brother's surprise birthday party, a good friend of mine got drunk and spent half the evening telling her and me that he had been hearing her name for fifteen years, and we should cut the crap and tie the knot. In the car I turned to her and said, "Look, are we gonna do this or not?" So we are doing it. This summer, I'm leaving New York and moving to the Rockies, a compromise on both our parts. I do not give a damn about her money, and she doesn't give a damn about my lack of it. Neither does her family or mine.

So you have three people who were made ecstatically happy by what Ang Lee and Annie Proulx's works of art set in motion. I haven't felt this good, this clean and directed, in many years. My life will never be the same. Nice, isn't it?

And the people around me ask me what happened, why I am alive again. I credit this directly to the *Brokeback* Effect.

===

I got engaged, hat over my heart and ring on her finger this weekend in front of half of Wyoming. I called her "little darlin" when I slipped the ring on.

Last night she said she's writing a thank you letter to Ang Lee, because she knows *Brokeback* is what made me finally move my arse!

Jack Schilling, 51, is a horticulturalist/garden designer who lives in Denver, Colorado. Brokeback_1 *is his screen name.*

Twentieth Anniversary

—Kerry Hibbitts

My earliest recollection of "gay stirrings," and looking back now, I recognize them as such, is from the second grade; I recall a vivid dream involving the boy who sat next to me coming to school naked.

I had my first taste of freedom at graduate school in Oklahoma, where I still live. After being here for a while, I heard rumors of gay bars. I was too scared to go; I was a stranger in a strange land.

In late 1985, I finally got the nerve to pick up a copy of the local gay paper. I saw personal ads in the back. I paid for a three-month ad, which first ran in the January 1986 issue. I waited nervously for responses. Nothing. Then I did something that changed my life: I kicked myself in the ass and said, "Don't just sit and wait; answer someone else's ad." So I read through the February ads, and the one just above mine sounded similar to mine. I wrote to him with my phone number, and he responded, suggesting that we meet. As that Friday night approached, I was extremely nervous waiting for him to arrive at my apartment—I was finally about to meet my first for-sure gay guy!

When he arrived, we sat and talked for a while, then decided to go get something to eat. After we returned to my apartment, he asked if I wanted to join him and some of his friends Sunday afternoon for a movie. It would give me a chance to meet other gay people. He told me to meet him at his apartment and we would leave from there. We were sitting in his apartment talking, and two other people came breezing in: one was his roommate, and one was their best and oldest friend. Three days later, I received a call from the old friend.

We chatted, and I agreed to go out with him. Two months later, we became partners. And here it is, twenty years later. Things have been great, and we've been happy, but like most couples, gay or straight, you settle in, life becomes comfortable and routine, and you start taking what you have for granted. That's where we were.

Then along came *Brokeback Mountain*.

Like most people who have shared their reactions here, it sneaked up on me about two days later. I would wake up in the middle of the night with scenes and music from the movie in my head, weeping uncontrollably.

Emmylou Harris's song "A Love That Will Never Grow Old" jumped out at me instantly. It haunted me.

My partner and I were approaching our twentieth anniversary, hosting a dinner at a caterer-friend's house. I had secretly brought along the CD. I had printed up the lyrics on a card with a picture of *Brokeback Mountain* in the background. After dinner and several toasts—all of which were reducing me to an emotional basket case—it was my turn. I told everyone that I wasn't great with words, and so would let Emmylou Harris speak for me. I passed out the cards and, through my already streaming tears, sat next to my partner as the music started. By the end, I was weeping uncontrollably and holding my partner. I finally gained enough composure to look around, and saw everyone else standing and crying. Even the caterer said later that she had stepped into the next room to cry. It was the most perfect night of my life.

Brokeback Mountain has made me more appreciative of the good thing I have. I'm much more physically demonstrative to my partner. I'm so thankful that I found my love. But more importantly, perhaps, it has opened a new chapter in my life regarding my friends and family.

I bought four copies of the DVD, one for myself, and one each for my sisters and mother. When I returned to Texas for my nephew's college graduation, I gave each of them their copy, along with a card explaining how the movie had touched me deeply and how I hoped they would watch it and be just as deeply touched. What their response will be, I don't know. Here I am, fifty-one years old, and I feel happier and freer than I have ever felt.

Kerry Hibbitts is a 51-year-old medical physicist who lives with Brock, his partner of twenty years, in an historic home in Oklahoma City. He usus as his screen name tex_in_ok.

Self-Acceptance

—Davis d'Ambly

Has *Brokeback Mountain* given you hope and made joy more possible? I know it has for me. For instance, my partner and I have definitely found a new spiritual center and a more joyful expression of our relationship. I also feel more able to share myself at a deeper level with others. That's part of self-acceptance, I suppose.

Fifty-eight-year-old Davis d'Ambly is an artist who lives in Pennsylvania with his partner of twenty-six years. He posts using the name Dave In Philly.

Evaluating My Life

—Sam in Chicago

For me, an out, urban, forty-three-year-old gay man in a nineteen-year relationship, *Brokeback Mountain* has affected me in powerful, surprising, and sometimes paradoxical ways. To start with, I've rarely felt so close to any character in a film or story as I do to these two guys. They won't get out of my head. This is the haunting quality that so many people have referred to. After watching the film the first time, I felt completely spent, weak, and numb. The second time I watched it, I was even more of a mess, unable to hold anything in for the last half of the film.

I read the story after that, and at the end of it had a good, cathartic cry.

In the subsequent hours and days, I began to evaluate things in my life vis-à-vis Ennis and Jack and what they went through. On the one hand, their story makes me feel lucky—it has shown me that things have been so easy for me, and that I should I appreciate everything I have.

On the other hand, it makes me feel like a coward for not being bolder about living my life fully, as who I really am. Since it has been easy for me, why didn't I do more, try harder, have higher expectations, rise to challenges rather than just settling or making easy choices in my life? Other people have said it, and it's true—*Brokeback* has made me realize the triviality of so many things, and has made me want to distill my life down to what is important and essential.

Sam is 43 and lives in Chicago.

A Choice to Change

—Mimo

Experiencing *Brokeback* is like having the most effective and successful therapy possible. For the first time in my life, I realized many things about myself that I had suppressed. And I thought I was an open out gay man with no issues! I discovered the Ennis in me.

I saw that I've been in complete denial and realized how I had been systematically closing myself off from the world, from people, from allowing any love in, or out, for that matter. I saw that I have a choice to change things, and that, if I don't, I could well end up like Ennis. I was heading in that direction. So I have made a choice to change.

===

It has given me the courage to call my ex-boyfriend and say the things I had been afraid to say; I couldn't bear for either of us to die without saying them. For a bit of background: we were together for seven years, and we broke up five years ago. When I saw *Brokeback* for the third time, I took my ex. Seeing the movie the first time prompted me to reconnect with him: I realized that I had started to hate him because I was afraid of being hurt.

We both experienced so much emotion; afterward we went and sat on the square together, arms around each other, saying those things we had never said. The tears were rolling down, and we didn't give a damn what anyone thought.

It was the most complete love I'd ever experienced before or since. It has given me the courage to open a new dialogue with my family. It has given me the courage to reach out to my friends and open myself up. Most of all, I've stared my deepest fears in the face and begun the process of freeing myself from them.

Brokeback Mountain gave me the courage to do this. It does not mean we are going to get together again, but it does mean that I will not deny any longer the love we had and the friendship we can have.

Life is richer already; there is a new spring in my step and a smile not just on my lips but in my heart. It doesn't mean that the world is suddenly perfect, but it sure is a hell of a lot better than it was.

The ice that had hardened my heart has begun to melt, and a torrent is rushing down that mountain. God, it feels good, and it may well have saved my life. Thank you, *Brokeback Mountain*.

Michael (39) is a dancer, a teacher, an author and an agent who lives in Sydney, Australia. Mimo *is the name he uses online.*

Living Openly and Happily

—Joetheone

My partner and I had been dealing with lot of emotional issues the last few months of our eleven-year relationship. *Brokeback Mountain* has helped me start communicating with my partner, my parents, my friends, co-workers, and complete strangers.

It has made me look at myself and recognize all the positive things in my life. I have been hiding and not letting people see me for who I am; instead, I was sort of still in that closet. Well, the last week I have not been in the closet at all, and when others talk about their husbands, wives, and children, I have started talking about my partner and the foster children that I helped raise, who are now adults.

Yesterday, my partner and I drove to Niagara Falls to be near the great force of this magnificent site. We sat and talked. He has been worried that my obsession is out of control, but he has attended every showing of it with me. On the way home, we both decided we had to see it again. I started crying when the Focus Features circles appeared, and I did not stop until the end. The entire movie was blurry.

It was the first time that he has put his arm around me and showed me affection in public. Strange, but he comforted me in public in a theater with fifty people. It felt nice to be acknowledged in public, especially since earlier in the day, when I asked him to kiss me when we were at the Falls, the way all the other people do, he resisted and walked away.

On our way to the parking lot, I felt so weak from emotion that he kept his arms around me and held me. It was wonderful and sad at the same time. Some young people saw us and said, "Look, there are two fa**ots." Well, that brought out the Ennis in me. I defended our lives, and they jumped in their car and took off. I told my partner I thought they were afraid that the tire irons were coming after them. That brought on the laughter.

Today P. and I drove to see my parents for lunch, and we discussed the movie. Mom said she was happy that this movie has brought us closer and made it possible for us to communicate more. We still have a lot of work to do on our relationship, but opening this line of communication that I thought in January was dead is a good thing.

My father just e-mailed me and said he was proud of the man I've grown up to be. I called and thanked him. He started to cry and said that he truly understood me after seeing the movie, and he wants to support me for as long as he can.

For Valentine's Day, we have always gone out to dinner with two lesbian friends. But this year we made sure that the other tables knew that the bill was for the two women and the two men, not for two heterosexual couples. It felt wonderful to do that small thing. There was no reaction really, and that is a good thing. The point is that I want to start living truly and openly from here on out, and if the tire irons come and get me tomorrow that is okay. At least I will have lived happily up until that point.

Joe is 42 years old and comes from Erie, Pennsylvania.

Things Unsaid

—PatSinnot

I appreciate the people in my life much more than I used to. I don't let trivial issues put me in a bad mood anymore. I tell my partner that I love him, and am much more affectionate with him. I also wrote a Mother's Day card to the mother of one of my childhood friends and told her how much her love to me as a child was appreciated. I am not going to let things go unsaid any longer, and what used to be taken for granted on the subject of love in my life now has much greater significance.

Pat, 50, is semi-retired and lives in Dallas, Texas. He has been with his partner, Jim, for twenty-six years.

Re-examined Life
—Fish

As a middle-aged, married man, this story and movie have made me determined to re-examine my career and my job. I don't love what I do any more, and it's time for a change. I need to take a look at opportunities and see what I could be missing. I'm also determined to reconnect with old friends and strengthen the friendships I have. I'm more of an Ennis type, and expressing emotion is difficult for me. I want to tell my wife and my kids more often that I love them. I want to hug my friends and tell them how special they are to me.

Forty-four-year-old Mark lives with his family in Pennsylvania and is a manager in a high-tech industry.

Gay men were not the only ones whom seeing Brokeback Mountain *forced to confront partnership problems—straight women were shocked at the intense sensuality they saw in this relationship between two men, and found they wanted it—or wanted it back—too.*

Relationship Is Most Important
—Christina

I'm a mom of two, in my mid-thirties, dealing with a toddler and kid stuff. I'm married to a great guy whom I started dating when we were nineteen and in college. The first thing I felt when I left the theater was that I missed that intense love in my life and wished we had more passion in our marriage.

I sat down with my husband and said we have to make some changes. He knows my obsession with this movie and story, and jokes about it, in a nice way, all the time. He hasn't seen it yet, but knows his time is coming. I even tell him that if it takes the love of two men to bring passion back into our lives, then that's the way it has to be! Anything to get him to notice the situation!

It's important to make your relationship the most important thing in your life, before the kids and before your job. I have a tendency to focus on the kids all the time, and he focuses on his career. The saving grace for us has been the simple things: calling each other during the day, having a weekly date night, and constant reminders about what we both want and need. Guys need reminding of what makes us happy. Well, at least mine does.

Brokeback Mountain has changed my life more than anything I can remember.

Christina is a 36-year-old stay-at-home mother of two from Portland, Oregon.

Marriage Needs Passion

—Passion

When I first saw *Brokeback*, I questioned whether I was happy. After a month-long evaluation, I decided I am happy but need to get some passion into my marriage. After eleven years with the same gorgeous guy, we have gotten comfortable and need to make some changes. Many of us married women have been asking the same questions. This has turned into a process of self-evaluation for many of us, which is good. Everyone needs to make changes in their lives, and if this movie has sparked it for us, it is a good thing!

Passion is a 38-year-old stay-at-home mom who uses her Master's in organizational psychology to manage her husband and two children.

Saved My Life

—mcnell1120

I, too, have lost that spark. I don't know why or how it happened. I turned forty this month and have been married for fourteen years, have two beautiful children, a house, two dogs, and a white picket fence . . . yeah, you name it, I have all the things in life I thought I needed. My husband got his Master's, and I've been in this job for sixteen years.

For the first time I looked at our marriage; we both did, and realized that we fell through the cracks. We used to have all sorts of wild sex; we broke a waterbed once.

What happened? Life is what happened. We Americans live our lives on the go all the time. I have to be here; you have to be there; Junior needs to be over there.

Seeing this movie brought out so much that I was not ready to handle. It made me think that life is so precious. It passes us so quickly. I took my friendship with my girlfriend for granted, and now she's gone, the only true friend I ever had. My kids are growing so fast, and I'm not taking the time to enjoy them.

I have been trying to get my husband to see the movie. I want him to connect. I don't like to nag, so I will wait until he is ready. But we did have our first intimate talk last night in a long time. We both admitted we need each other. We are still in love. But it could go bad if we just let it go. This movie gave me courage and opened my eyes.

I am so blessed. I've said it before, and I'm going to continue to say it: *Brokeback* saved my life. I truly believe that.

Nellie, a 40-year-old married mother of two from Chicago, is an insurance adjuster who loves painting and photography. She posts under the name Mcnell1220.

Grateful for the Experience

—Jaysmommy

I am feeling such longing, something I have not felt in a long time. I have a good life. I'm forty-three, a healthy woman with a fine and dear husband of eight years. I have a wondrous three-year-old son and a close relationship with my mom. I've been fortunate to earn a decent income for most of my adult life in a business that I love. But this film has stirred in me some deeply buried and confusing feelings.

Before *Brokeback*, I knew I was in a rut, both emotionally and physically. The routine of daily living—the juggling act of parenthood, career, and family pressures—combined with, I must admit, a bit of lethargy on my part, had created a void in my life that I didn't know how to fill. My marriage was in coast-mode: we shared emotional intimacy, physical affection and good communication, but the steamy passion of the early years was lacking. I was taking some small steps in an effort to bring some excitement back into my life and marriage: exercising regularly, eating healthy, and making better choices.

And now *Brokeback Mountain* has opened me up completely. It has accelerated this personal journey I had already begun. I have fallen in love with Jack and Ennis's love for each other. I am incredibly aroused. I want to reach for my husband, yet at times I feel the need to isolate myself with this re-discovered erotic longing. One minute I'm begging him to see the movie with me, the next minute I want to keep these feelings of yearning and desire all to myself, as if I have entered into an imaginary love affair with Ennis and Jack. How can this be?

I am still on my journey, and I do not yet have the answers. But I am less afraid of the road I am on. All the emotions that flooded over me for the last month, as a result of *Brokeback*, were at times terrifying and always intimidating. The questions raised about the choices I've made, the second-guessing about what might have been had I followed other roads, the fear that I've made mistakes that cannot be rectified were all overwhelmingly frightening at times. There have been moments when I wished I had never seen this film; I thought I would have been better off without these weeks of angst, sorrow, and confusion. But that wish was always replaced by a sense of gratefulness that this experience was given to me, that this door to my own soul was opened.

If I can overcome the fear of looking deeply into my heart and exploring both the light and the dark within, then I will be able to heal and be a better person, a better friend, a better mother, a better wife, a better daughter. I want to make my tiny little corner of the world a better place if I possibly can, and in order to do that I have to make sure my spiritual house is in order. The gift of *Brokeback* is the release of the mental shackles that inhibit my progress toward this end.

I know there will be bumps along this road. I know there will be times when I feel locked up again. When that happens, I will think of Ennis and Jack and recall what might have been for them and rejoice in the beauty of what they did have together. I know in the end that the sorrow will be replaced, once again, with hope.

The Brokeback Thing To Do

—DeTina

No one I know wants to talk about the movie as much as I do, which is understandable, because it's been months since the movie was out. The movie has helped me a lot—and I am straight! It helped me enjoy my hubby more, and sometimes when I'm thinking of doing something that is probably not in my best interest—even just stupid little stuff like eating crappy food—I think, "That's not a Brokeback thing to do," and then I feel less like I need to do it. What I like best about Brokeback is that the reason that I like it, as a straight person, is unclear—so I'm enjoying thinking about it, mulling it over, learning about myself, about the world around me, about love, as I ponder this movie and my and others' reactions to it.

Stoke the Flames

—Alma

I'm a heterosexual married mother of five kids. This movie changed how I see my marriage. We've always had a good marriage, but after *Brokeback*, I saw how important it was for me to cherish my partner and to not take for granted the freedom we have to live and express our love, both verbally and intimately.

As I looked at the happiness that Ennis and Jack shared through infrequent but powerful times of intimacy over the twenty years of their friendship, I thought about all the marriages I know where the partners are humdrum and bored and lack passion and appreciation for one other. Jack's death at thirty-nine is a reminder not to assume that life will be long. *Brokeback* is a wake-up call to remember how precious it is to find the one great love of your life, and to cherish it: to stoke its flames and to care for it.

I feel like I just woke up from a long sleep. I feel haunted by the idea that life is half over for me, and I am suddenly aware of how grateful I am for the treasure of my man, who is still sexy, caring, deeply committed, and my best friend.

Julie, 45 is a married mother of five who lives in the Midwest and is a professional writer and business owner. She uses Alma *as her screen name.*

Reckless Abandon

—MyLeftArm

I'm thirty-nine, female, totally heterosexual, and totally re-in-love with my live-in boyfriend since seeing *Brokeback*. Jack died at my age. Ennis was left lonely, with important words never said and with deep regrets at my age. If I am going to have a life partner, I am going to be like Jack and love him to the point of reckless abandon. *Brokeback* showed me what fear can do, and I don't want to have those regrets. It's better to be hurt, even die, like Jack, than to live with regrets like Ennis. This is in no way a put down to the Ennises out there. We Jacks love you. But we've got to live and to love.

Lisa, 40, lives with her boyfriend and seven pets in New York. She is a gay rights activist and member of PFLAG. She uses MyLeftArm *as her screen name.*

29 Wake-up Call

—EnnisinIdaho

I am a thirty-three-year-old man. I have been married for ten-and-a-half years, and I have four kids. The last eight months of my life have been turbulent, and I think that's why *Brokeback Mountain* has had such an impact on me. I have lived like Ennis all my life. I was born into a Christian family that lived by the Book—literally. And I have grown up doing the same, but all the while having an internal struggle that I had always hoped would go away. I have secretly liked guys all my life. I got married to a nice girl who actively pursued me. Marriage was expected; to come out to my family would have been the most disastrous thing I could do. We were perceived as the perfect family—I am one of five children—and I was not going to bring shame to the family.

In the summer of 2005, my wife and I took in a single friend of ours to help him get back on his feet. He was much younger than me. I loved him like a son, but I had to be careful of my feelings, as he was very good-looking and fun to be with. My marriage had been pretty dry for years. I am not romantic and have a hard time trying to be. My wife was unhappy and turned to this guy for comfort. To make a long story short, she recently gave birth to his baby, a son, Gage, whom I will raise as my own. Gage's biological father loves him and hopes to be a part of his life in the future. It is difficult for me, as all the feelings of the affair come back to me. But I love Gage as my own as well, and have to live with the fact that I will not be the only daddy in his life. I am adjusting to that fact. It will be okay.

Gage is wonderful: so full of life! He is a beautiful boy, the spitting image of his father, who is beautiful too, by the way. He is very playful, and he and I are bonding. I love him so.

In comes *Brokeback Mountain*. I was in shock. There have been boys and men in my life that I enjoyed being with, but never to the degree of Ennis and Jack, definitely not as intimate. I have always wanted that with a man, and there was my dream, displayed so beautifully on the screen. I couldn't believe it! This movie rocked my world. It shook me to the core, so much so that old baggage that I had been carrying for so long finally loosened enough that I had to drop it and look at it.

After many counseling sessions, much pain, and looking into my life and my wife's life, we decided it was best that we divorce. During our counseling sessions, I revealed to her that I had a thing for men, and that I had felt this way all my life. But we decided to try to maintain a friendly relationship, for ourselves and even more for the children. I moved into our spare room.

We broke it to the kids about the divorce. The oldest took it the hardest. She is doing better now. I plan to stay in the spare room for a while, as we do not have enough funds for us to live apart. We are working to clear up the bills so that I can move. This will also give the kids a chance to get used to the idea. We are already joking about who will live with whom, pretending to get offended when the kids choose the other parent; it's all fun—right now. I expect to move out in the spring, if we can make it that long. But my wife and I were best friends first, so we are relying heavily on that relationship right now. It is a painful, but necessary, process. I can say that *Brokeback* had a huge hand in making me realize that I have been living a lie for my thirty-three years, and it's about time I take a look at what I have built.

My wife found a link to the *Brokeback Mountain* Forum online . . . and found me. At first, she was angry that I had kept the Forum a secret. But she decided to read my posts. She had always grappled with the details of how I felt or was feeling, why I said the things I said, and questioned my true feelings on our situation. Reading my posts, she said she felt as if I was someone she had never met. I don't blame her for being angry. But as she read, she felt she understood me better. We will always be best friends. We have just come to the realization that we must go our own ways, whatever they are.

I find depression knocking on my door regularly. Life is hard right now.

I have been thinking tonight about the people—friends—I may lose because of this "new me." It tears me apart, for I cannot think that they will take it lightly.

I already told a young friend of mine, someone I know from church, about the divorce, and he went off on what it will do to the kids and on and on. He lost his dad to suicide two years ago, so I know he is speaking out of his pain, but now he is asking why things went wrong in my marriage. If I told him about me, I don't know what he would do. I love him—he is a great guy, and I don't want to lose his friendship. It would be painful. I am so afraid of being alone; that is my worst fear.

I love my family and would do anything for them. This is a struggle that I have been wrestling with for many years. To my way of thinking, that the reality that has only ever existed in my mind might see the light of day is crazy. Yet in it, I see freedom. I told my wife that I have no intention of running out and finding a mate or starting to go clubbing, doing the "gay scene," or anything like that. I think some things have to heal in me for me to be able to fully love someone in the way in which I was intended.

Sometimes, I feel terrible for the path I led my wife down. She didn't ask for this, and if I had been honest from the beginning, my life would have been different these past eleven years. But honesty back then wasn't an option. I hope someday I'll be able to forgive myself for that. Luckily, we had some good times and four wonderful kids. And I plan to make more memories with them, just on a different level. For my wife's sake I decided to tell my family the whys of the divorce. She has taken much blame from my family because of the affair last year.

During her pregnancy, my parents even told her, though I did not agree, that she needed to put Gage up for adoption and that I would probably never love this baby as my own. My being closeted has been the thing that kept me from being the husband I needed to be. She turned to someone else for the love she never felt from me. I do not want to play the blame game, but she feels that, at least to my parents and siblings, I need to come clean and own up to my part of this failed marriage, which involves outing myself. I am willing to own up to my part; I have no problem with that, but I am nervous.

If nothing else, *Brokeback Mountain* calls you to action. If this movie awakens something in you, you have to act. My eyes have been opened.

===

July:

I sent an e-mail to my family alerting them of my divorce, and I came out to them. I come from a loving family, but a very religious one as well. I was not sure how everyone would take it. I didn't expect to be shunned, but I felt ashamed that I would be seen as embracing a lifestyle I had been told was wrong and against God. I do not see my family much, maybe twice a year. But I didn't want them to think badly of me. I have my many nephews and nieces whom I love as well. All have responded with support and love, referring to the divorce, as I interpret it. That they can handle. That they can accept. But the gay thing? They won't accept that so easily.

===

August:

The family and I were at a picnic last night. As we were walking around, my wife said, "I bought you something." I asked her what it was, and she looked at me and said, "A movie." There are a lot of movies I want, so I was not sure what she was talking about. I guessed a few that were wrong. I looked at her and by the expression on her face . . . "*Brokeback?*" I said. Yes. I was in shock! I couldn't help but laugh. She said it's a bit of a peace offering and a way to show her love and support for me. I could not believe it. I still am in shock. She is a wonderful woman. I hate that I have hurt her, but she is strong, and she will always be my best friend.

I wanted to share that with you guys. I asked if she would watch it once with me. She said that even though she hates it and would probably cry when Alma sees Jack and Ennis kiss, she would watch it, just once.

Like many of your partners, my wife had about ten minutes of comments and that was it. She doesn't know that I am still reeling from the film.

Well, I guess I will leave it at that! I'm so glad this Forum is here—a bit like a *Brokeback Mountain* Hospital! I'm not sure when I'll be discharged, though! I might be here for a while!

So, please keep me in your thoughts and prayers as my wife and I get the divorce papers rolling soon. Now that the decision has been made, she just wants to get it done!

I cannot stop saying thank you to you all. As much as you think of me, I think of you! I can't wait till I'm at a place where I can return the favor and help someone else here.

EnnisinIdaho is a 34-year-old audit controller from Idaho.

Jack I swear...

30   No More Beans

For some Forum members, Brokeback Mountain *was a catalyst in a more general way, helping them to find a courage previously unknown, a courage that permitted them to stand up for gay rights, or overcome difficulties at work, or just to move on, in various ways—in the words of Jack, "No more beans!"*

Brokeback in Academia

—gary74

Some of us academics have been so affected by *Brokeback* that we have changed the course of our research, teaching, and general thinking. Four of us will be writing in the film studies journal *Screen* this year about the film. Two of us are gay men, professors from the UK. The other two professors are women, one straight and one gay, from the US. I will be writing about gay spectatorship in relation to crying, the closet, and melodrama.

Academia is one of the careers where being gay and out can be a plus, in the United Kingdom, anyway. Many students have come to talk to me about *Brokeback.* I am passionate about the film, and it makes me proud to be able to write about it as part of my job. This will be the foundation for a book I am going to write as my next monograph. I hope others in my field don't attempt to write about *Brokeback* without understanding how precious this film has been for us. Academics can be bad about that.

By the way, my office at work is a *Brokeback* shrine these days. Do I care what people think? *Na*

Gary74 is a 32-year-old man from Notting Hill in the United Kingdom.

What I Need

—paintedshoes

Brokeback Mountain allowed me to come to terms with some issues in my past, but somewhere, lurking in the back of my mind, I knew there was more; I just couldn't find it. In the last few days, I have pieced together my thoughts, fears, and needs, to explain to myself what happened to me.

It was after reading the story three times, searching my soul long and hard, and facing what I knew to be the truth, that I made a radical decision: I quit my job after nineteen years! I can't believe I'm putting it in writing. I'm staying on to wrap up some projects, but I'm out at the end of the month. I'm looking for a job, though no prospects yet. I'm divorced, fifty-seven years old, with two kids and five grandchildren, and I did the stupidest and bravest thing I may have done in my life.

I can't live in misery for fear of what the future may hold, not anymore. I am laughing to myself, at myself because— though on some level I'm scared to death—I feel a lightness of heart that I have not felt in forever. None of you here made my decision for me, but all of you here enveloped me in love, compassion, and understanding. You helped me to come to terms with myself and what I need for myself, not for what I thought other people expected. Bless you all.

Jackie, 57, is a medical laboratory technician from Maryland who is a mother of two and grandmother of five.

Intensity of Goodbyes

—bgriffith

I'm a gay man in a thirty-two-year great relationship.

As a child, being gay, I learned to reflexively stuff my feelings away. At first, this was how I dealt with my reactions to men. But eventually, this became a way to deal with any and all feelings. My rational mind assumed the driver's seat, and I could intellectually bull my way through any situation. Feelings simply became something to brush aside. It was not only my reactions to men that I was able to rationalize, but other areas as well, such as my work.

Then came *Brokeback Mountain*; it destroyed my defenses against my feelings. I spend a lot of time nowadays just sitting around listening to my heartbeat; it has returned me to that basic level of existence, perhaps because I haven't done that in so long. I am a professional nurse, and the change in my level of dealing with my feelings has required me to retire. You may imagine that, in a critical care unit, situations arise that might excite feelings. I have successfully dealt with these issues for fifteen years. I can no longer do this, and this week I retire, with no regrets. It is just time, and this amazing film has been the agent that has pointed my way to this resolution. It was never going to be easy to make this particular change, but the magnitude of the feelings that *Brokeback Mountain* has unmasked rivals the intensity of the many goodbyes that any retiree experiences.

The Politics of Being Gay

—Heather Ferguson

I am a lesbian in a twenty-one-year relationship. We fell in love like Jack and Ennis, so innocently back in 1985, also declaring, "We're not lesbians—isn't it weird that someone might think we are?"

We had been taught that being lesbian was gross, sick, perverted. So, in the midst of a beautiful, affirming, life-giving love, the word "lesbian" didn't fit. Neither of us had ever known an out gay person.

I have been out with family, at my faith-based workplace, at church, in the neighborhood, at our kids' elementary school, everywhere, for two decades. But I left the "politics" of being gay to others. Now I know I must do more. And I am. In fact, the anti-gay right has brought their war against us right here to Minnesota. They want to constitutionally limit the definition of marriage, and all legal protections, to mixed-sex couples. The fallacy that same-gender couples undermine society strikes at the heart of the truth borne out by my life.

So I have joined with others. We are organizing those who identify as spiritual or religious individuals and communities of faith to stand against the proposed amendment in Minnesota. I find strength for my work from *Brokeback Mountain*, because it is the clearest, most prominent cultural statement to date that our same-gender relationships are about a love that beautifully and profoundly changes and uplifts the two people it joins together, love that fills the couple so full that it spills out to touch and uplift others.

Heather Ferguson, 40, and her partner of twenty-two years live in Minneapolis, Minnesota with their two sons. She uses Prayerofthanks *as her screen name.*

Power to Love and to Act

—Betty Green Salwak

I am a long-married, Christian mother of two. It's been three months since I read the story and was shot through the heart. I have lost twenty-seven pounds and countless "productive" hours of activity. In my own life the story hasn't finished yet. Annie Proulx says, "It is my feeling that a story is not finished until it is read, and that the reader finishes it through his or her life experience, prejudices, world view, and thoughts." I don't know yet when this part of my story will come to a happy ending. It may be a long time.

Even though there have been painful revelations, I will not return to the person I was before. *Brokeback's* gift to me is a new power to love that was hidden too deeply to express. My radar for other's pain is at an all-time high, and I find myself reaching out even to strangers.

But I have been compelled to act, also.

I have just finished training as a pastoral lay minister; I want to be available to those affected by AIDS. My brother died almost ten years ago, and this is how I can show my love for him in a way that lives on. I hope to bring my voice to the silence I met with years ago when he was ill. I have asked our senior pastor to consider *Brokeback Mountain* for our next series of movie nights.

I love the person I have become because of *Brokeback*. So now I cry.

Betty Greene Salwak is a 52-year-old Sunday School director who lives in Indianapolis with her husband and two teenage children. Neatfreak *is her screen name.*

Brokeback Mountain held up a mirror to many lives—and then broke it. As viewers carefully studied the pieces, they reflected on their own understanding of the lessons of the movie, lessons that sometimes cut both ways, but were, in the final analysis, beautiful.

Openness

—John Tate

How powerful the message of openness is in the film—it's as if the countryside sits there in the background mutely crying, "Look around you, Jack and Ennis. Be like me, open yourselves up." It's up to the audience to fulfill that command. I'm trying my best.

John Tate, 38, is a psychology student living in Brighton in the United Kingdom. He posts under the screen name Redbrit.

Seeds of Inspiration

—Sheera Duerigen

In seeing what Ennis and Jack had, and what they lost, I came to understand all that I have and all that I was about to lose. I was on a quick road to losing myself. I had been heavily caught up in my own negativity and was letting it reign free.

My change began as a simple movie viewing and branched off into so many more things. I began downloading fan mixes, which re-invigorated my passion for music, in turn giving me the confidence to take up singing again. I read fan fiction, which planted seeds of inspiration in my mind and has compelled me to begin writing once more. I devoured the stories of the transformative impact that this film has had and realized that it is okay for me to go through a catharsis and regeneration. I have made friends who have helped me to realize that I deserve love and that, in fact, I should expect nothing less.

Brokeback Mountain has been my lens to see the flaws, the cracks, the missed opportunities, and all the steps backward. But, more importantly, it has been my lens to see the triumphs, the beautiful silence in between where inspiration germinates, the blessings I have received, and, perhaps most poignantly, the endless potential that lies within me and within all of us to give and receive "a love that will never grow old."

Sheera Duerigen is a 20-year-old college student from the Bay Area in California. She uses Sheera *as her screen name.*

Personal Renewal

—Hayek_uk

Emotional upheaval creates an opportunity for change and personal renewal. Psychoanalytically, the depth and intensity of the emotions triggered by all aspects of *Brokeback* is like a collapse of the strength of the ego: all the old ways of doing things, old beliefs, old patterns, old justifications, old certainties. When it happens, whether we know it and analyze it or not, we can sense how powerfully wonderful and liberating this experience of "ego collapse" can be. Perhaps this is part of what we are experiencing.

Ego collapse is an essential precursor to major personal change. It may occur only once or twice in a lifetime. When it happens, people often do not recognize it or deliberately turn away from it. Maybe this is what Ennis did.

But ego collapse can be an opportunity to discontinue beliefs and behaviors that are no longer worthwhile and strike out with confidence and hope in new directions. The window of opportunity does not remain open long: the ego rebuilds and quickly becomes rigid again. Even if things have been changed somewhat, they are likely to get frozen at an intermediate stage

With *Brokeback*, we feel a dramatic internal revolution, revisiting with great clarity and emotional force seminal episodes and periods in our lives. But then what?

There are lots of things we can suggest with some thought, but thought is not enough. It has to come from deep in the emotions, experience, and intuition.

Perhaps we recognize instinctively that we need to intensify and prolong the *Brokeback* experience if it is to prove beneficial. The film tells us clearly what not to do, what not to continue doing, or at least the price that will likely be paid for doing so. But the positive change we need to replace it with is not obvious, and it is not the same for everyone. Each person has to find his or her own positive change before the opportunity to act on it closes off.

So the wonderful, deepening, and shared prolongation of the Brokeback experience, while new possibilities can still be discovered and adopted, feels much better than trying to break the addiction prematurely.

Charlie, 49, is a professional political scientist from the United Kingdom. He shares his life with his partner of 15 years. Hayek_uk is his screen name.

Liberty

—Matteo Z. Ferolie

*B*rokeback has unleashed things that have been cruelly bound for way too long. The Liberty Bell inscription reads: "Proclaim Liberty throughout the land unto all the inhabitants thereof." *Brokeback* is a new ringing of that bell.

No wonder you feel as though your path to life and enlightenment has been brightened! After a few days, I felt my gay self invigorated. I felt more positive about my identity than I've been in years. My beliefs, too, were fortified, and I felt challenged to put self-doubt behind me and to accentuate the beautiful parts of my male soul: my kindness, my caring and concern for others, my love for my fellow men and women, my sensitivity to my surroundings, my love and reverence for life.

Matteo Z. Ferolie is 65, retired, and lives on Staten Island in New York. He posts using the screen name Zadoc.

Legacy of Abuse Destroyed

—valkyrie

After I saw the movie the first time, I was stunned and could barely talk. Images and scenes flashed through my mind. I could hardly sleep. And then it started: waves of pleasure rolled over me, sometimes like lightning flashes sizzling through my body, again and again, the whole day and night and well into the week. I kept seeing the love scenes repeatedly with my inner eyes. And I started feeling aroused most of the time. Sometimes I cried from grief and pain, but then the pleasure waves started again.

With the help of a good friend, I was able to sort out what was happening to me. I realized that a part of my body that had been frozen was beginning to thaw. Deep inside me, as well as in the whole area around my hips, I had been frozen ever since I was a small child, a legacy given to me by violators doing things to me no children should ever experience. It happened from when I was young until my teenage years. Those who are inclined to trespass the boundaries of children can sniff out a broken child like hounds, and they went for me.

There were many of them. Luckily for me the main offender died, and that saved my life. Others who did not trespass turned a blind eye. I never knew love, tenderness, being held, being cheered for whom I was. I could not protect my body, but I protected my Self/Soul, hiding it deep within my own body. They took my body, but I could not let them take Me. So I froze my body to lessen the impact of the tearing agony inflicted upon me. Thus my body remained frozen, for many years.

Filled with self-loathing, shame, and self-hate, I started on my life without abuse, but I had sworn to myself to take revenge, and the best revenge was to learn to love. I would not succumb to dealing with life the way my trespassers did. A long journey it has been, through ups and downs, through therapy, education, having a child, friends, and therapeutic massage. I have gone from abysmal loneliness to being where I am today. I have learned to love myself, being able to give and receive love from friends and family, loving my child endlessly.

Brokeback gave me all of my physical body back. I am not frozen anymore. My body is open and free-flowing, a new experience unsurpassed by anything I have ever known. It is as if the whole hara area has been awakened: my life force, my aggression, and my sexuality. By aggression, I mean the force in me that can stand up and protect, that pushes forth and up and that will attack if threatened, something I haven't been able to do before. I have so much energy that I run when I'm going up and down stairs. Joy is welling in me, and I am sexually ignited by the littlest thing. I find I love to drive big cars with big engines; I dream of racing. I play music so loud my teenage daughter complains. I see all these good-looking guys out there, no longer viewing all men as potential rapists. I'm free to love men now. And I love women.

Wonderful. I feel so alive my whole body tingles. The love and sex in *Brokeback* was the trigger, and I feel like a bottle of champagne, when the cork slams into the ceiling and the champagne is flowing. The fluidity of love and sex appeals to me. What matters most is the person; the gender of that loved person is an added bonus.

I experienced adolescence, young adult, and midlife stages in one shot, and I wouldn't have had it otherwise. Better late than never. It is never too late to reclaim your own life.

Wall Comes Down

—Conny

I've been hiding behind my big concrete wall for the last eight years, not letting anyone in, besides some friends who have the key, not being totally miserable, but not happy either.

I knew I had to do something, so I started therapy again, called my hypnotherapist, and went into regression. With his help, I went through my whole past, felt the pain from forty-three years of abuse, pain from lost loves, and not being the girl I wanted to be. I dealt with that pain and healed my inner baby, child, teenager, and woman and started healing my self.

And all of this in a period of two months!

I started a search for my *Brokeback* love from twenty years ago, found her, and recently made contact with her. It was good hearing her voice and talking to her, but it also made me realize I have to let go and move on.

And so, last week I signed myself up on a Dutch lesbian site. Maybe nothing will come of it. I'm not directly searching for a woman, but it felt good to post my profile; I'll see what happens.

So far, a lot of changes, and I'm feeling so good and proud.

Conny Voesenek, 43, a dog walker who lives in Ijmuiden, The Netherlands. Her screen name is Conny.

My Best Friend Ever

—Juliacat

Yesterday, I went to the pub with my ex, with whom I am now best friends. We saw *Brokeback Mountain* together the first time.

I remember that when we got out of the theater the only thing we could say was, "What a masterpiece!" But I'm sure that he, like me, was already beginning to feel the power of the emotions about to explode. I had invited him for dinner. We went to my apartment hardly speaking, and then it was like a seaquake: we had a terrible row and he went away, slamming the door. When we lived together as a couple, we never had such rows. I know that his anger exploded that night because of the film: many of our misunderstandings and old problems came up again. He had a few stories about being with men that I totally understood and accepted, and the last thing he shouted at me before going away was, "That is the kind of love I'm desperately looking for. I'm not talking about gay love. I'm talking about love!"

This happened one month ago. Obviously, he still blames me for having not been able to love him any longer. That was the reason we separated two years ago. But I did not know that it still hurt him that much.

Yesterday, we were together at the table of the pub drinking beers and talking about politics. I don't know how it happened: perhaps the beer helped me to forget my reticence about talking, because I talked for more than an hour. It seemed that I could talk for days. I went on and on, talking about this Forum, about the weight in my heart, about what Ennis and Jack mean to me, about how strong and universal the message of this film is, about how much it affected me and still does. He sat there listening, nodding, almost always silent, with a few questions here and there. When I stopped, he said, "Catia, that's more words than you've spoke in the past two years. This film got you good. Now go on and ask yourself why you're not able to love anybody any longer. Don't stop here."

He called me this morning: "I feel melancholic. I think I'll have to see that movie again, though I don't want to fall into it like you have. I know what it's about. I know that hunger and thirst for love. But I'm so happy that you're my best friend, and that I will never have to read on a postcard that you're no longer here. This friendship is a treasure, and I know I'll never lose it."

I said to him, "Now you need to look out of the window and find that love you deserve. I'm here to help."

Brokeback Mountain can help us explore our inner selves.

And I've been able to talk about it with my best friend ever.

Catia F. is a 40-year-old legal secretary and ardent cat lover who lives in Rome, Italy.

Straight Cowboys Get Lucky

—Ruth

I've been feeling pretty devastated as of late.

This may sound odd, but weirdly enough, a movie about a relationship between two men has contributed to my recovery greatly! It's bizarre and I can't figure it out. The heat generated from the movie screen, getting the chance to read this

Forum, sharing in everyone's stories, squealing and giggling: it's amazing therapy. And my awareness of myself as a sexual being . . . well, I kind of feel like my pilot-light has been re-ignited! (*Woof!*)

How strange is that?

I'll be in Montana next month—got family there—and them cowboys had better look out. It cracks me up that some folks are all offended by the content of *Brokeback*. In all likelihood it'll cause more straight cowboys to get laid than any other movie in history.

Ruth, 42, comes from Seattle and is a freelance cartoonist, artist and animator.

Not As Bad As I Thought

—RickB

*B*rokeback Mountain has cured me, as only a good religious experience could. I'm known for my gloom and doom, but *Brokeback* has rocked me to the core like nothing before. I haven't felt depressed since I downloaded the trailer last fall. Sadness maybe, but with happiness standing strongly beside it. If I ever do get depressed again, I will listen to the soundtrack, face the sadness head-on, have a good cry, let it all out and feel the weight lift. I am in love with this whole experience. I've read that the high of a new love can last about a year, so we'll see. I can't help feeling that I'm not the same person I was before all of this started. I feel like the past has been wiped away. And for the first time in a long time, I feel that life is not as bad as I thought it was.

Rick is a 49-year-old composer, artist, and daydreamer from Hollywood, California.

Living for Dummies

—Steve Lindholm

Nothing in my entire life has ever hit me so hard. Jack and Ennis have opened the door to my emotions, which had been closed for so long. And they've allowed me to feel what real love must feel like. I was straight and married for seven years; after that, I had a gay partner for fifteen years, but no love, just settling.

Now I feel that I deserve to know what real love is. But at sixty-one, same age as Ennis would be now, I fear it's too late. This empty, aching feeling that began with Jack and Ennis, seems like it has me at a tipping point. One way, I'm starting to die, and one way, I'm starting to live. If I'm dying, I must put all my feelings back in the bottle, try to forget the glimpse of love I felt with Jack and Ennis, try to numb myself to this incredible hurt, and get back to my going-through-the-motions life.

If I can actually start to live a real life, it's hard to know where to start. Does anyone have a copy of *Living for Dummies*? Maybe it's not too late, and I can finally know how it feels to love. If this is possible, I have to reach out—I swear—to make it different. But I don't know how to reach out in the right way. I need to be more open, but if I let too much spill out, it'll be overwhelming—too needy—and I'll scare people off. The truth is, I don't know quite what to do, but I'm working on it.

Steve Lindholm lives in Michigan, where he runs a specialty gift shop. He is 62 and divorced. He uses Strazeme *as his screen name.*

The Cowboy Myth

—johnbeene

The truth is I've been changed. I look back at who I was when I breathlessly watched the trailer and listened to "The Wings" for the first time, and I see that I am different now. There's something extraordinary about being able to pinpoint that moment of change.

And there is more change to come as these feelings work their way from the inside out. Sometimes I feel things moving inside me so strongly—walls and buttresses collapsing—I half expect to hear my joints popping. The most important thing about *Brokeback* was not its commentary on the consequences of the closet, which is what I think most gay men who've seen the film relate to first, but its re-examination of the traditional construct of masculinity.

As a gay man who grew up feeding and corralling cattle, building fence, and working summers in an oilfield roustabout outfit or in an auto repair shop, I have to say that, deep down, Jack Twist makes sense to me. The bedrock of my personality—my identity—was laid down in those hard places and those quiet times. *Brokeback Mountain* put me back into contact with my soul. It is helping me to become more honest. Ultimately, it will make me more whole.

Brokeback Mountain has much to say to men about how often the regime of masculinity demands the beating human heart as a sacrifice.

Brokeback allows us gay men to declare false and folly the rigid, reactionary tyranny of the cowboy myth, a myth that Hollywood has coddled and perpetuated. We can be emancipated from this myth.

The truth is the mythical Hollywood cowboy is emasculated. The real cowboy finds his manhood in the freedom to say who he is, to be who he is, to make his own way.

Brokeback requires a man to do work. It is honest work: the work of opening your heart and exposing it to the cold mountain air, laying yourself bare as the ice-scraped rock. Few have either the desire or the ability to do that kind of work. You have to be brave. Bravery is a virtue in limited currency.

Who among us is brave enough to lead?

From my vantage here on the Mountain, I see vast territories to explore. I see that there are trails through the Great American Desert laid down long ago. And I see it passes through the peaks.

Go west, young man. It is our destiny to be better than we are.

John, a chemist who loves hiking and cooking, is 38. He recently moved back to Boulder, Colorado, after several years away. Johnbeene *is his screen name.*

The Person I Understand Better

—Christine Wilson

My son had several girlfriends, some quite serious, but it was only when I saw him with A. that my husband and I realized that he really loved him. It has been so good for us to see that he has this capacity to really love someone. To me, he is just my son, who happens to love a man.

Like everyone else, this film has got me good. I went to see it to help me understand my gay son, but you won't be surprised to hear that the person I understand better is myself.

Christine Wilson, 59, is a scientist who lives in the United Kingdom. She posts under the screen name of montezumae.

Indescribable Sunrise

—Mike Mattingly

The last three months have been unique in my life and I intend to enshrine, not forget, this experience. About midnight last night I began the task of reviewing and printing out all relevant *Brokeback Mountain* communication for inclusion in my scrapbooks.

It is now 10:00 a.m., and I have been doing this nonstop for ten hours. So many friends sent such touching notes. Even though I have known some of these guys for 10 to 25 years, I have never shared such emotional things with them. Their willingness to expose their feelings has been a magical thing. *Brokeback Mountain* has changed my entire life. It has provided me with the richest emotional experience of my life.

Today around 7:30 a.m., as I was printing, the most indescribable sunrise in all the twelve years since I moved here presented itself—the final gift! It will be like this, "just like this, always," if only we all believe. They can never take us back into darkness because we are finally free.

Mike Mattingly is a 46-year-old married antiques dealer from Kentucky. He uses Suffused *as his screen name.*

31 A Separate Peace

—Mejack

Shackled to the seat, my ankles hurt from the rubbing of the leg irons. Five hours in the prison bus, seven or eight men, feet linked together by a chain, hands cuffed. The barred bus windows covered with wire mesh were cracked opened a little, while the Florida late-summer sun beat down unmercifully.

I'd heard about Raiford, that hellhole with its chain gangs, and the abuse. It was the Deep South of 1954. I was seventeen and about to become the youngest guy in Florida State Prison. I was alone, and so afraid!

The first iron gate slammed shut behind us as we drove through. A few yards further and the second gate did the same. The bus door opened. A guard removed the chains and herded us through a doorway, down a long corridor, to a large open place.

"Welcome to New Cock Court," he said. Years of prison slang had given the name to the holding area for new arrivals. Oh God, why do they call it that? I wondered.

"Take off your clothes. Everything." Trembling with fear, stripped bare, I stood there, waiting. "Open your mouth." "Raise your arms." "Bend over, spread your cheeks." Not knowing what to expect next and, without warning, the thrust of two fingers began the body cavity search. A communal shower removed the delousing substance from my skin. I stood there naked, terrified. What was happening to me, only three months after high school graduation?

At the distribution desk, prison clothes were piled in my arms. "Put these on." The opposite door opened. The long passageway through Cellblock E was lined with locked cells. Faces pressed against the bars, leering at the newest entry from New Cock Court. My ears were ringing with the raw, obscene remarks and gestures, as I was led to a cell down near the end.

Two walls had bunks, three high. There was a combination sink/toilet with no seat. The four men inside said nothing. One motioned toward the empty top bunk. I climbed the ladder, and lay there, afraid to move. They left me alone.

After a while, a buzzer sounded. "Chow!" The man who had pointed me to my bunk said, "Stay by me. You'll be okay." There was a kindness in his voice. All the cell doors opened at once. I stayed next to him and kept quiet, hoping to remain unnoticed.

After chow, we returned. The doors would stay open for two hours of free time. Quickly, I retreated to my upper bunk. My newfound protector sat on the lower bunk and read his book. I would be safe, at least for now. Soon it would be lights out. Oh God, what then?

He closed his book, stood and brushed his teeth at the sink/toilet, and said, "How's it goin' up there?" Suddenly, lights out. Within seconds, he was in the bunk with me. I pleaded, "No, please, no." "It's either gonna be me or all four of us."

Five days and nights of hell.

Then, suddenly, a guard appeared and took me out. The judge had made a mistake, hadn't noticed my age till it was too late. I was too young to be here. Guys my age were supposed to go to Apalachee, the place for youthful, first-time offenders. They transferred me that day.

I arrived in the late afternoon. A bunk in B Dorm was assigned, and a guard escorted me to the chow hall. It was civilized, two hundred young men eating, even laughing.

At free time, after dinner, I saw Billy. Walking down the sidewalk toward me, he nearly took my breath away. Billy was twenty, good-looking, all slender and muscular, with curly hair and blue-green eyes.

He must have noticed my reaction, because he came right up to me and introduced himself. With a broad smile, he said, "Hi, I'm Billy." Somehow, with those few words he took the hurt away. He knew how afraid I was that first day.

Though somewhat inexperienced, I had always been attracted to guys. It wasn't that way for Billy. Nothing in his experience had prepared him for someone like me. Yet there was this bond. We both realized it that moment, and for the next two years we were inseparable.

The guards monitored everything. There was free time each day for a couple of hours after dinner. Billy and I always went down to the field to lie in the grass and talk. We shared our innermost feelings and our dreams, occasionally touching our fingers together or looking into each other's eyes. That's all we could have. And we would never let a day go by without saying "I love you."

In the mid-1950s, even in prison, nobody had a boyfriend except Billy. Well, and me. Everybody knew about us. All the guys were straight, as far as I know. They probably assumed Billy was too, and that I was the queer one. Maybe they were right.

On one special afternoon, we were all hanging out on the steps of one of the two dorms, maybe sixteen or eighteen guys around, with no guard in sight. With no television and no magazines allowed, the guys were living vicariously through Billy at that moment. They started chanting, "Kiss him, Billy, kiss him," urging him on. Billy slowly stood and pulled me up beside him. He whispered, "Do you wanna do this?" Before I could answer, or even think, he wrapped his arms around me. I never knew until then how much he really wanted to hold me. Then he kissed me, a full, open mouth kiss. It seemed unending. It was our only kiss, ever.

I heard them . . . "Holy shit, do you believe that?" "Damn!" "I ain't never seen nothin' like that before!" We sat back down. I couldn't let go of Billy's arm. Suddenly, somebody said, "Y'all shut up. Guard's coming." And it was over.

The next day I asked Billy about the kiss. He joked and said, "What kiss?" Then he got serious and said, "I'm glad it happened. You okay? You still love me?"

"Yes, Billy, I still love you."

Before the kiss, the other men were just looking for some entertainment. It was almost like a double-dare. Afterward, the reaction was one of awe, I guess. We took a risk, and they knew it. Within a few days, the guards got wind of it, and started asking questions. Of course, nobody had seen anything! One guy asked me, "When's it gonna be my turn?" But it was just light-hearted humor. Later, a guy called me "gal-boy" but someone quickly corrected him. "His name's Paul."

Billy and I were treated with respect. But it wasn't for being gay, or because of the kiss. The respect was there because we never hid how we felt. We admitted our relationship to all, and we had dared to do the unthinkable in the face of harsh punishment if we had been caught.

Not long afterward, I was at work in the prison office and got word that Billy had been in a fight over at the brickyard where he worked. He never told me what the fight was about. He was sent to the hole—solitary confinement—concrete floor, one blanket, and minimal food. I was filled with anxiety for Billy's sake.

Next day a guard got smart with me and said "Whatcha gonna do now that your boyfriend's in the hole?" Without thinking, I replied, "Fuck you!" He grabbed me and said, "I guess you wanna go down there with him, huh?" He unlocked the cellar door and marched me past Billy's cell, down to the end of the hall and clanked the door shut.

Billy yelled, "What the hell did you do?"

The guard said, "He wanted to be with his boyfriend." That's the only time Billy was ever angry with me, angry that I had put myself in such a situation.

A day later they came and let Billy out. He had been in the hole for three days. They kept me the maximum twenty-nine days. The guards were sure that I was the queer, and Billy was just being taken in. So they let him out to make my punishment worse. When I came out of the hole, I was pale and thin. That was the only time I ever saw Billy cry. That evening, the other guys were watching to see what we'd do. We walked down the sidewalk together, right past two of the guards, into the field and lay on the grass again and talked and loved each other.

I loved Saturdays. Work was only until noon, and the rest of the day was free time. Billy lived up the hill in A Dorm, and the sidewalk led down to me in B Dorm, and on past to the ball field. After lunch, a shower, and a change of clothes, we'd have the whole glorious afternoon.

One day at our place on the grass, Billy was on his back, watching the clouds, one arm behind his head, the other stretched outward. I moved over some and laid my head on his arm. He said, "You're gonna get us in big trouble." But he didn't move his arm. Little intimacies. Yeah, I loved Saturdays.

I asked Billy once, "Ever think about sex?" "Umm," he answered. "How 'bout you?" "When I think about it," I said, "I think about you."

He was quiet for a long time as he contemplated. He had so little experience to draw from. I can't even imagine what odd pseudo-hetero image he must have conjured up in his mind. He just said wistfully, "Hell, that ain't gonna work!" But being in love isn't only about sex. Good thing! Like Ennis said, "I ain't yet had the opportunity" to be a sinner. But we had intimacy—and lots of time to love.

Billy had another year and a half to go when I was released. Parting day was unbearable. And it was against the rules for us to correspond. I went to New York to start life over. Two years went by, and I had no idea where he was. But I knew his home was in Griffin, Georgia, so I went there, located his mother, and found where he was staying. Of course, I was unexpected and Billy was confused. He had a new girlfriend, Ruth, and they were getting married. The three of us had lunch together, and when we said goodbye we tried to hide the tears.

A year later, I called again. His wife Ruth answered. Billy was back in prison, this time for five years in Georgia. She was going across the state the following week to visit him and asked if I wanted to go along. I did.

My sweet Billy sat across the table from his wife and me. What must have been swirling through his mind? He talked to Ruth and, all the while, under the table, entwined his feet with mine.

We never saw each other again.

It was twenty years before I could get through a day without thinking of Billy. Eventually I met a sweet girl, we married, and had four wonderful boys. With loving father/son relationships and a happy marriage in every way, thoughts of Billy slowly subsided. He faded into an old memory, never really forgotten, but never brought to the surface either. Until *Brokeback Mountain*.

Suddenly, after fifty years, all those emotions came flooding back into my mind. If only I could see him one more time. If only I could know where he was and what his life was like. I began searching. I had to deal with this thing. One thing was sure, though. No matter how much I wanted to find Billy again, I would not let it affect my family; I wouldn't give up a good life for a dream. But if I could learn a few things—was he alive? was he okay? was he happy?—if I could just know that, hopefully I could put this all aside again, and go on with my life. Yet, there was a part of me that wanted Billy.

Memory fails so easily. When I try to visualize his handsome facial features, I find they've faded somewhat in my mind, like an old photograph. I have no photos of Billy. His parents visited him once and took pictures of us together, but I never saw copies of them.

I drove 650 miles round trip to Billy's high school in Georgia, just to look for his picture in an old yearbook. When I got there, I found the yearbooks for those years were missing.

Who would have guessed that the school librarian would be the key to my search? When I told her Billy's name, she said she thought he might be the grandfather of one of the students at the school.

Soon after, I received confirmation that Billy had passed away several years ago. I could hardly stand it. There was so much I wanted to say to him. I feel so utterly alone now. I never had to grieve before.

Billy's wife, Ruth, lives in Atlanta. I called her. She was cordial, remembered me from years ago, and invited me to come visit. At first I declined, but she insisted.

My tears would not stop. My wife noticed, but I shrugged it off. She knows nothing of Billy. How do you explain to your wife that you're going out of town to meet another woman who was the wife of the man you've loved for fifty years?

I flew to Atlanta to visit Ruth. We had met forty-eight years earlier. Our conversation began with family. Billy and Ruth had a son, a daughter, and two grandchildren. We spoke of my family and then of Billy's death thirteen years ago, of pancreatic cancer. He was fifty-eight when he passed away.

I could feel those damn tears welling in my eyes. I had to say something, explain somehow. "Ruth, I've got to tell you about Billy and me." "No, Paul," she said. "I already know."

She began:

"The first time we met, you flew from New York to Atlanta, and you didn't even know Billy's address. I thought that was odd. Why would you go to such expense to look for Billy, and just stay one afternoon?

"A year later you called. Billy had been returned to prison. I planned to visit him and asked if you would like to go with me. To my surprise, you did—another expensive trip for only a couple of hours with Billy. We had visited before, but this time there was a tear in Billy's eye. I knew it wasn't for me. We sat across the table and talked, but he couldn't keep his eyes off of you.

"Years later, back home, I asked him about you. He leaned back in his recliner and said you were just a good friend. But then he got misty-eyed again, said it was his allergies.

"When Billy was in hospice, we knew there were only days remaining. We spoke of many things. Then I threw caution to the wind and said, 'Billy, do you want me to get in touch with Paul?' At first he was startled, but he realized that I knew. He answered, 'No, I wouldn't even know where to find him.'

"A couple of days later, I went into his room. There was an envelope in his hand as he slept. When he awakened, I asked him what it was. He said, 'If Paul ever comes, would you give him this?' I told him I would. Billy died three days later."

Ruth reached into her purse and laid the envelope on the coffee table. It had been in the safe deposit box until yesterday. As I picked it up, I could feel Billy's fingertips in mine. My hand trembled. And the tears came again.

"Maybe you should take it with you and read it later," she said.

As we were saying our good-byes, Ruth said, "Paul, tell me something. How often did you and Billy see each other?" I replied, "The last time I saw Billy was that day when you and I visited him." Now it was her time for tears. She said, "But I always thought . . . ." Her voice trailed away. We parted as friends.

Back in the hotel room, it was so hard to bring myself to open the letter. It was my only link, my final contact with him. After this, there would be nothing, ever again. Finally opening it, I saw that it wasn't a letter at all. Just a little slip of paper, with a few lines that I will treasure forever . . .

Paul,

The sweetest days of my life were spent with you.
Go find some grassy place again.
Lay you down and close your eyes.
I'll meet you there.

Billy

My search has ended. Finally, I have been able to lay Billy to rest in my heart.

Epilogue
October 20, 2006

It has been seven months since I learned of Billy's death. Today I visited his grave and came face to face with that stark reality. My friend Widge (WDJ) met me in Atlanta and we drove together to the cemetery. The anticipation of this day had consumed my thoughts for weeks. During the journey we spoke about Billy and I could barely contain my emotions. When we arrived, we just sat a few moments in the car. Widge offered a quiet hug as my heart trembled within. We walked, searching. Then there, right in front of me was the marker, my Billy, my very soul. The flood of tears came once again. At that moment, oh, how I wished I could just lie down beside him once again. The grass was soft and green. How perfect. I think I hear his voice: "Go find some grassy place again, and lay you down, and close your eyes . . ."

How fortunate I am to have the shoulder of a friend. How thankful I am for *Brokeback Mountain*. Without the film, I would never have begun the search for Billy. I would never have known nor read his last words to me. Now, finally, I have been able to "put things in their place."

Paul Mejack, a 70-year-old retiree from Florida, enjoys traveling with his wife. He posts under the screen name Mejack.

32 Proud of Us

—BradINBlue

I have finally broken through. Thank you Ms. Proulx, Mr. Lee, and every soul that unleashed this epic upon humanity. *Brokeback Mountain* has brought an end to the tumultuous and painful journey that has been my life.

I grew up in a mind-numbing environment among vast ranches, broken-down pickups, the twang of country-western music, and the incessant wind of eastern Oregon. My daddy, a good man, worked hard and tried to build a life for me and four siblings, while my mom drunkenly eroded every striving. A plumbing contractor by trade, dad found it hard to fulfill his dream as provider in such surroundings and sought work in a more urban part of the state.

While he was away, setting up to move us with him, my mom hooked up and moved in a son of a bitch truck driver, who had only one thing in mind: drunken, loud, violent sex with my mom, with us kids cowering under the covers a thin wall away. Through the booze and the bruises, she finally saw a glimmer of light in my dad, and one night while the son of a bitch was on a long haul, she packed us up and we escaped hell. My daddy took her back, and things got better despite the scars that I believe determined my life.

I managed to dust off, but not eliminate, a brutal childhood, which I blamed on eastern Oregon—a place. High school years were tough. I had girlfriends, played the macho role, but I cherished more than anything the close bond I had with my best friend. We did everything teenage best friends do, but always together, without our girlfriends. He got married, and to this day, I know he had the same longing bond with me that I did with him. Following suit, I married "the prettiest, sweetest little gal" in Oregon. I was nineteen. Life seemed good; she glowed, deeply in love with me, but I was missing something.

I got a paramedic certificate, and partnered up with a guy who was so much like me, my mom couldn't tell us apart. Working twenty-four-hour shifts together, we laughed and wrestled and shared and I know we fell in love, but this love was unspoken. When our shifts were over, we went our separate ways—me back to my wife and him back to his bumpy relationship with his soon-to-be wife. I longed for the next shift, just to be with him. A year went by, and I knew what was between us was wearing him down. In that time and place, he and I weren't in the cards. Both of us were Ennis del Mar. He wanted kids and normalcy, so our partnership ended.

On the surface, the relationship with my wife was that of two young, beautiful people living the good life, dressing in Polo, driving the best cars, traveling and playing with other couples (I found myself longing for time spent without wives and with other male friends), and being the envy of most everyone. Behind the closed door, she longed for more affection and romance than I could muster, and at twenty-two years old, the Hawaii trips and the jaunts to Nordstrom's were more than our two jobs could cover. In debt, unhappy, and terrified, I decided to venture into the great unknown.

My initial experience was mind-blowing: initially positive, then deeply negative. For me, the blue eyes, jet-black hair, long eyelashes, and chiseled, stubbled face (yeah, like ol' Jack), and all with not the least hint of a lisp, destined me for way more than I could handle. All the attention, all the opportunities . . . .I submersed myself, all the while trying to maintain my marriage. The toll was heavy in sorrow for my wife, who desperately wanted kids. I finally said goodbye and moved to the city. I was quickly eaten up by the lifestyle—lots of crippled critters. I was sought and even stalked but, it seemed, not for my heart but for fifteen minutes and a cigarette. Attempts at relationships ended in disaster. I was a man who wanted a man, but I became convinced I wasn't going to find him. The lifestyle, the attention overload, was too much and I ran back to the closet.

I finished college while working full time at my paramedic job and decided on a career change. I was hired as a police officer, and the Maker added not one, but many, chains. I couldn't possibly be a male cop and be whatever it was I was.

To the 'burbs, away from it, and back into the arms of my wife—a decision that to this day I am so sorry for. It worked for a while, but the aching and longing grew. I sought solace at first in porn, then in infrequent randomness—hell, at least I was finding there were men out there, most of whom were married or closet-locked. I was determined to remain, but it was my wife who fled. By myself, I was a tight angry fist.

Trips north to Seattle almost every weekend. Out of sight. Same crap. I was going nuts. I was twenty-nine going on seventy. Then I met a friend there. He was way out—no lisp, but he felt he had to make a point. We had fun on his motorcycle, we romped about the wet city, and he made me comfortable, but I knew I could only do it there. He fell in love with me; I fell in love with his ways.

The day before New Year's Eve plans with him, I was holed up in this smoky hellhole of a bar waiting for rush hour to ebb before starting my northern trek. This place was next to the freeway and had a reputation for attracting the over-fifty desperates. It was away from the other bars and scenes, so I could duck in and out without being caught by my comrades in blue. The place was full, and the cold wind was howling outside. I got my Bud and headed for a dark place in the corner, out of sight.

Beer half gone, the crowd parted, and through the smoke there stood the most handsome cowboy I ever laid eyes on—his hat, his buckle, his coat, his boots. Our eyes locked, and he gave me this half-cocked smile that still brings tears to my eyes. I was stunned.

I looked away and gulped at my beer, but his gaze never left me. I finished the bottle and made my way carefully to the bar for another. His stare followed me, and I was scared to look at him. Now standing next to him, I bought the beer, looked into his gorgeous blue eyes, took hold of the lapel of his lined Levi coat that looked new, and said, "You get that for Christmas?" He smiled, and it was off to the races. Steve. We drank, we laughed, we shared. He told me about his horses and his business. He owned a restaurant, and his employees had insisted on dragging him to such a place as that bar. I told him what I did—I was a cop—without a flinch and why I was there. I would have to be leaving soon. More beers, traffic became light on the freeway, and then I didn't care. When the kiss came, it was hard, heartfelt, and genuine.

The smell of him on my pillow the next day, the memory of him pouring his lean muscular frame out of his jeep after the trip up the hill behind me, and the half-cocked smile on his gorgeous face, ever so slightly scarred by an old motorcycle accident, embedded themselves deeply in my soul. Would this be it? Did I remember him saying his mom would be staying with him for a couple of days, and then he would call? No number left.

I stayed in for three days. I slept embracing the pillow with his scent. I thought of nothing but him. Then the phone: it was Steve. I thought my heart would burst out of my chest. We talked for three hours. From that phone call, we were inseparable.

I would stop by his restaurant while working, he would make me a huge burger, and we would sit upstairs chatting and staring into each other's longing blue eyes. Later, I slipped my business card under the wiper of his Jeep, "Thanks for the burger, baby . . . Your favorite cop" scrawled on the back. He was content with who and what he was. Past relationships had left him wondering if there were men out there who could fall in love with men and not be a part of that lifestyle of freewheeling sex, open relationships, and the scene. He worked hard, and we talked about buying horse property.

He found us that horse property in rural Washington State. A long commute for me, but when he took me up there, it was breathtakingly gorgeous, even under two feet of February snow. Ponds, creeks, fenced and cross-fenced, old broken-down trailer house—but we scraped and made it happen. We ditched the trailer and got us a real nice doublewide we'll build when we retire. Paradise. Live happily ever after? Not by a long shot.

The Ennis in me, like the Ennis in Ennis had he not let Jack drive off there in Signal, would be a wedge, and for me it was. People are staring. They know. I'm not one of them. The rural setting helped, though. It was away from the city I worked in, and nobody knew me up there—yet. Steve got a job running the local logger bar, which had a reputation for Friday night fistfights and beer only, on draft or in the can. We both joined the volunteer fire department and immersed ourselves in the community.

Because we were both black Irish—same dark hair and blue eyes—folks assumed we were brothers, and we went with that. With him behind the bar, and me going fishing and spotlighting deer at night in a drunken haze with the locals, we fit right in. We were safe and secure as brothers, but—when I went to town for my four days of working—not a mention to anyone about my personal life. Some on the police department, including my best friend, knew my ex-wife and assumed I was between marriages. I maintained two lives, personal and professional, with distance between the two.

My daddy died suddenly and literally in the arms of my mom, who had finally seen the light—two years after Steve and I stole away. He told my mom, "I think Brad is finally in love," and when she shared this with me after he was gone, I wept. He was one of eleven, raised in vastness with a dad not unlike that of one Jack Twist. My daddy and Steve, in those two years, were two peas in a pod separated only by time.

The years clicked by. I had what I had dreamed of, but the stigma, the bullshit, and the childhood pain were still there. I turned to compulsions, as if I had to have something going on the side to survive. Drinking, gambling, pornography, attention and desire in those bars . . . this proved disastrous for our relationship.

He left me twice, the first time while I was working out of town for a week, with a note: "I don't know what's wrong, but there is this wall between us, and I can't deal with it." Promises of change. He moves back. Same spiral. Second big move: Grandma died, and he's gone to California to live on her spread. One whole summer, me broken and crying. While he is gone, there are no compulsions. What is wrong with me? Blame it on the Maker.

Steve is so alone, as am I. This love is like that of Jack and Ennis, once in a lifetime. After letters of promises, he gives in, and I go a-fetching. I lay eyes on him at the airport in San Jose, and I want to grab him and hold him and kiss him and say, "Son of a bitch," and I see it in him too, but I can't. What would people think?

Leading up to a third, and certainly final, breakup, I decided something had to give with me. I won't let him in, but why? By now, we had forged friendships with folks in our rural community. They adored us, had to know what we were all about, and we both had families who accepted and loved us unconditionally. These were huge hurdles and we were over them. Our attempts at forging friendships with other gay couples were futile. To them, it was all about open relationships (sex), and we weren't comfortable with that.

I put this crap on the table and promise Steve I'm a-changing. It is good, but not real good. The wall has not lifted, but is certainly not of concrete. I tell Steve I'm going to a cop barbeque. He says fine. I say, "I want you to come." He looks at me like I just lost my mind. My stomach is in knots, and I feel like throwing up. He says he'll find something else to do. I take a deep breath. "I want you to go with me." He gives me that cocked smile I fell in love with and tells me he'd love to go.

"This is my partner, Steve," I say. Not a worry, not a leer, not a snide comment. They are more comfortable with us than I am. Going home, I was riding high. What have I been doing for the past eighteen years?

The new and improved me was upon us six months before the *Brokeback Mountain* debut. Still, something was missing.

What happened as this thing unfolded in front of me was like nothing I had ever experienced in cinema. I slowly inhaled this story, and once inside, it wrapped around and clenched the core of my existence and would not let go. I burst from the theater after the last frame and into a men's room stall, gut-punched and sobbing. I'm walking to my truck, and for the first time in my life the feel of the unusually mild January breeze, the sounds, the people, and the sights around me penetrated my soul. That last vestige of a wall that kept all this and Steve at arm's length was completely gone.

I drove home in a state of euphoria. I had been vindicated in celluloid. Yeah, the tears were there, and the longing for Ennis and Jack to break through and have a good life, but that was 1963 Wyoming! This here is about Steve and me in 2006—a once-in-a-lifetime "love that will never grow old." It has nothing to do with Gay Pride parades and bars and games and random sex. It is about us.

The next day, I took Steve to the movies. He didn't say much, but that night was the beginning of what should have been the past eighteen years.

No fears, no chains, no notches, and no fake smiles—they are a thing of the past. I am so proud of us and, finally, of me.

Brad B. is a police officer who lives with his partner Steve in the rural Pacific Northwest. He uses BradInBlue *as his screen name.*

Afterword: Beyond Brokeback

—Michael Flanagan

Time for post 4000.

This week when I was up in Vancouver, I was asked what I thought the Forum was about because it wasn't necessarily about the film anymore. I think this is a good place to answer this because it truly has a lot to do with how *Brokeback* has affected me.

I've been out since I was a teenager, which was a while ago. I went through the seventies and early eighties going to bars and baths and got into a relationship that only lasted two years in the mid-'80s. Around that time, I got involved in AIDS activism. One of the questions that occurred to me then, and has nagged at me since, is where do I fit in the "gay community"? I really had no interest in going back to the bars and the baths—I never was very good at it anyway—and was in my thirties, which in bar culture means you're dead. Meanwhile, many of my friends died. Many, many of my friends died. I wrote for the gay press for a while, took gay classes, and got involved with film organizations; but all of that still left me wondering: where do I fit, both in the gay community and in general?

Then last December, this movie came out. Suddenly now, I have radically expanded the base of my friends. I've met men who have been in relationships for over twenty years and men who are just coming out in their forties, fifties and beyond. Even though the gay movement has always paid lip service to diversity, I've always found that it was the pretty and the young—and usually people who look like they were cast as extras from "Queer as Folk" or "Queer Eye for the Straight Guy"—who have been most valued, not folks from blue and white collar jobs—everyday folks. The ideology of the movement has always advocated coming out. However, if you don't conform when you come out and frankly, if you're past thirty and don't spend all your time at the gym, how can you conform to many of these stereotypes, then you come out to a void—to nothing. You become part of a community that doesn't want you and doesn't see you.

The Forum is a community where communication is the essential element. People are allowed to express their hearts no matter where they are along in their development, and that's a good thing. One of the reasons that Ennis was unable to move forward in his life was because he couldn't see where he could go or what he could be. What this place has given me is a place where I can be myself and see my way forward with people who are like friends and family to me, regardless of their gender, their age, or what they look like; and that's a really good thing—something worth treasuring. It's our own little "cow and calf" operation of the mind, if you will.

For me, the ability to be able to talk with people about books in the Book Club thread is an essential part of the building of community, an ability for me to share with others thoughtful communication and to get people interested in reading, which is a compelling part of my life. Also, the ability to just hang out with people in the Diner thread gives me a place where I feel accepted and where there is little expected of me but my presence. In the other threads I visit (Canadian threads and music threads), I get to hear information from people in whom I'm interested and share my own input. I don't go to the threads related to the film that often any more because I'm at peace with Jack and Ennis, and they deserve peace.

The reason that there are "no reins on this one" is that the capacity of love is limitless. I look forward to more time with you all, giving and taking as Jack and Ennis couldn't. In an earlier post I said that if only Jack and Ennis had had friends, their lives could have turned out so much differently. That's what we're here for folks, to be the people for each other that Jack and Ennis (and Alma and Lureen) didn't have.

Much Love,

Michael Flanagan

Michael Flanagan lives in San Francisco and uses MichaelFlanaganSF *as his screen name.*

Index

Symbols

1224butternut 34, 57

A

Alma 135, 191
amdaz 56
Amy 152
amymm 152
Andrews, Linda 134
Antony 91
Arethusa33 118
atruant 146
Aubé, Jean 16

B

B., Brad 222
B73 96, **97**, 98, 101, 102, 103, 106, 110, 116
Basqueboy 165
Baxter, Robert 41, 126, 135
BayCityJohn 67
bcatjr 99, 106
Beethovenrox1770 178
BenKing 11, 138
bgriffith 199
bluehorse 31
Bobby 171
Bobby19in1963 171
Boris 65, 153, 169
BradINBlue 222

brokeback_1 14, **179**
brokebackLJ 53, 164
BrokenOkie 32

C

Caron, Nelson 141
Carr, Doug 72
Casapulla, Sharyn 54
Catalina 96, 97, 101
Changedforever 12
Charlie 203
ChrisFewa 166
Christina 187
Cincydarryl 165
City Girl 52
Conny 206
Courtois, Wayne 35
couzins43 167
Cowboy Dave 32
Curt 69
Cynical21 102, 106, 111

D

d'Ambly, Davis 182
Dan 138
danac 30
Dave 142
Dave in Philly 182
Dean 56
Denney, Joseph 53
DeTina 191

M

mcnell1120 68, 122, 188
McNulty, Jim 12
magicmountain 29, 104
Magnan, Jack 136
mainebartender 67
Mark 187
MarriedMan 31
Mattingly, Mike 212
Meira 156
Mejack 213
Mejack, Paul 213
Michael 185
michaelflanagansf 228
michelle 81, 125
Mike80 36
Mimo 184
MindyM 118
montezumae 212
Moonbeam 52
Mooska 139
Mortimer, Jonathan 1
MSPJeff 79
Murray, Sarah 121
mwp2paris 35
MyLeftArm 192

N

neatfreak 42, 201
Nellie 68, 122, 188
Nelson 141
Nicole 15
NotBastet 99, 101

O

O'Brien, Carol 45
O'Neill, Michael 17
OnesEnough 164
Osprey 157

P

paintedshoes 199
Palaski, Lyle 139
Passion 188
Pat 186
PatSinnot 186
PennQuaker 10
Perkins, Michael 35
Peters, Jermaine 33
Pierre 51, 130
planetgal471 109
Plumtree11 102, 107, 108
Poohbunn 120, 152
prayerofthanks 201
Price, Lancelot 95, 99
Pulungan, Bianca 40

Q

quijote 124

R

Rance 157
Rebel 70
Redbrit 202
Richard 53
Rick 209
RickB 209
Rodríguez, Luis A. 165
royandronnie 40, 100
Ruth 208

S

Sagha/Mo 17
Salwak, Betty Greene 42, 201
Sam 183
Sam in Chicago 183
sarah 121
Schilling, Jack 14, 179

Printed in the United States
75764LV00004B/118-606